S0-BOL-027

To my family: you always make our house feel like home.

Sydney-based interior designer Darren Palmer is a regular columnist for *Australian House & Garden* magazine and has contributed articles to a number of Australia's premier home and lifestyle publications, including *GQ Australia*, *Luxury Home Design*, *Renovate* and *Grand Designs Australia*. For a number of years he has also been a judge on the immensely popular television series *The Block*.

In 2014 his first book, *Easy Luxury: An Expert Guide to Creating Your Perfect Home*, was published by Murdoch Books. The purpose of *Easy Luxury*, which went on to become a best-seller, was to make great design accessible to everyone.

After studying fine arts and design, and having a career as a graphic designer, Darren decided to pursue his true passion: renovation and interior design. He gained firsthand knowledge by successfully renovating a string of his own properties before moving on to learn from some of Australia's best interior designers.

Today Darren is one of the most sought-after and highly regarded designers in Australia. Through his interiors studio, DP Designed, he is known for creating designs that are accessible, comfortable, sophisticated and, above all, highly appropriate and individual.

Darren lives with his family in Sydney's eastern suburbs and is always planning his next renovation project.

10/17

HOMESPACE

HOMESPACE

CHANGING THE SPACE YOU HAVE
INTO THE HOME YOU LOVE

DARREN PALMER

Photography by Felix Forest

MURDOCH BOOKS

SYDNEY · LONDON

Contents

Introduction

Growing up in central Queensland in the 1980s, my reality was as nuclear and 'normal' as you could get. My mum and dad were paying off their house, built on stilts and on a sloping block in a newly developed part of Gladstone, a town with a population at that time of 30,000.

My older sister and I, two years apart in age, often used to play with our cousins who lived up the road. There was also two years age difference between the two of them and, quite neatly, the younger one was two years older than my sister. We had this great little reference point of perfect nuclear families with two kids, older girl, younger boy, all spaced two years apart in a perfect representation of Australian life in the '70s and '80s. We even lived in very similar houses only two blocks away from each other, so my normal life seemed very 'normal' indeed.

Home was nothing too grand. We had a bedroom each, one bathroom between us and everything was on one level. The kitchen was kitsch to say the least; memories of it still linger with its apple green benchtops and brown laminate timber-look cabinet fronts. It was cool when it was done in the late '70s, and strikes me still as a bold design statement.

Our home was immaculate – my dad always pays great attention to detail and had the walls perfectly painted in whatever colour my mother wanted at the time. We had polished timber floors and one of the most garish pink-apricot puffy leather sofas, which was put out to pasture only a decade ago.

It was home, and a really nice, comfortable and always well presented one. My mum and dad were there when we arrived home from school, we had meals together and basically lived a really happy existence.

We'd go to relatives' places for Easter or Christmas holidays and that's when I started to realise how different

everyone's places were. One aunt and uncle lived on a cattle farm in a big old dark Queenslander. There was plenty of space to run around and play as a kid, but the house itself was very different from my home. I loved going there because the rooms all connected to each other – you could walk in through one doorway and out of another, linking space to space to space. The kitchen was very simple and mostly freestanding, and it was OK to put anything down anywhere; it didn't have the sense of order our house had.

Another aunt and uncle lived in cotton country in New South Wales and their place was meticulously well kept – more so even than ours, I think, although my mother might not agree. Their bathroom had carpet on the floor; not a rug or a mat but broadloom wall-to-wall carpet. It might have been because of the cold winters, but as a kid I remember thinking how strange it was.

My grandparents lived in a little house that was older than my dad and had housed six kids in its time. There was a wood-burning stove that also heated water, and the whole place was just held together with nostalgia and love.

Through my experiences of visiting different places and seeing how people occupied their own domains, I discovered that there wasn't one 'normal' at all. Flash forward to my life now, and my family looks nothing like the 1980s Palmer home I grew up in. We have a son, three dogs and a cat – a menagerie that I think would easily expand if it weren't for our busy work lives and my hesitation to live with any more pet hair.

Our friends have one or two children, live in apartments or houses, have or don't have pets, or whatever it is that suits them best. I couldn't honestly say that anyone I know lives just like anyone else. There are so many different permutations of family life, from single mums or

dads to gay married couples, straight and unmarried ones, married couples with kids or with none. There isn't a family unit we call nuclear anymore, and everyone seems to run their own lives in their own way with their chosen places of habitation reflecting their lives, their families and their styles.

The more I've travelled the more I see that geography influences lifestyle just as culture does. In some parts of the world, the architecture is designed to wrap people up during freezing winters, whereas in tropical regions, you'll find outdoor pavilions for enjoying the easy, breezy lifestyle. I've seen villas, maisons and chateaux, apartments, mansions and homesteads. The beauty in seeing more and more places and being in more and more homes is the realisation that there isn't one answer to living, just as there isn't one type of family.

Home is where the heart is, but the place where you keep that heart can be very, very different from that of your neighbours or even your family. As I've said, no two families are alike and we have all created our own place to call home in our own image, which is why this book has come into being.

The homes I work on and the families I work with are all very different from one another. The results are also just as different, although there is always a common thread, an appreciation of the work I've done in the past and a desire to see what the result will be when my clients and I work together to create what is often the realisation of a lifelong dream – the dream of the perfect house, made to fit the owners, their family and their lives.

In the following pages, you will see differing levels of service, from full renovations to furnishings and décor, or a blend of the two. There are different types of homes; some are grand and some even grander. Each one, though, has a unique set of constraints and results, challenges and triumphs. Common issues are met with solutions cut to fit the fabric of the homeowners' lives. There are lessons to be learnt in how different people and different houses tackle the same design requirements with different budgets, different briefs and different results.

The idea to take away from this book, through the case studies and projects, is this: good design process, while fitting a different brief each time, is always going to work in the same way. (Although, due to the subjective nature of taste and point of view, design fundamentals can be adhered to with wildly varying results.) Hopefully, the problems you face or the design itch you have, might well have been scratched by one of the homeowners featured in this book. If not, there will still be plenty for you to learn along the way.

Beachside build

RESORT-STYLE LIVING

Opposite: Enormous doors disappear into a void, creating a seamless flow between indoors and outdoors.

The brief

A few years ago I gave a series of regular talks at Sydney's Coco Republic Design School. It was a great way for me to get in front of potential new clients. These lectures were about past projects, renovation, decoration, creating balance and layers, and making family-friendly, appropriate homes, and other general theories of mine.

At one of these talks, I was asked about my inspirations. I started discussing the importance of nature in informing my palettes in terms of colours, materials, textures and feeling. A lady in the audience came up to chat afterwards, and let me know that what I said really resonated with her. She went on to say she was very interested in the natural approach and told me about a house she and her partner were going to build in Sydney's North Bondi. She wondered whether I'd be interested in taking a look.

Dropping in to visit them at the site, in their house that was about to be demolished, I was taken by how easy they were to get along with. Both of them were a little older than me; she had retired recently and he worked away from home for months on end. They had no kids, no pets – it was just the two of them creating their ideal adult space to enjoy either on their own or with friends. They didn't have to worry about things like privacy from children, or everything being wash and wear or safe for kids – all those rules of thumb for a family home could go out the window.

The architect had received the same brief as me, and his draft plans were spectacular. What this family required was pretty different from what a family with kids would require. It was all about how two people can live comfortably, entertain when they want to, have guests to stay once in a while (but not for too long), have space for a home office, and for the house to be of such a design that the two of them can be in adjoining rooms – one watching a movie while the other watches TV – without disturbing each other. They generally wanted to live in a private, tropical beachside oasis. Some brief!

The client particularly liked the idea of feeling as if she was on holiday in a Balinese luxury resort. Now, one of my favourite places on earth is in Bali, a beautiful hotel called Alila in Uluwatu. I'd been there maybe six months earlier so I knew exactly what that luxury holiday brief should feel like. As you can imagine, I couldn't wait to get started. On top of that, she wanted a sense of tranquillity and for the spaces to be as voluminous as possible, working with the sweeping ceiling in the boat-like roofline.

All briefs have their challenges, as do all clients, but I've been lucky enough to be able to choose who to work with for a little while now. Clients have to understand what they're going to get out of working with me, what my aesthetic is about and what that means for their home. A good designer has a distinct style that can morph to create bespoke interiors reflecting the desires of each client. These clients were no exception. Lovely people, easy to work with, with very few set-in-stone ideas. These really are the best jobs and we set about deciding on the parameters to work within for this home.

Below: Sandstone reclaimed from the original house on the site was used for retaining and feature walls.

Opposite: A curved ceiling, inspired by the waves on nearby Bondi Beach, draws the eye into the house.

The client particularly liked the idea of feeling as if she was on holiday in a Balinese luxury resort.

Opposite: A lounging platform cantilevers over a pond outside the master bathroom.

Structure

A FLEXIBLE LAYOUT

The existing house had too many problems to make it worthwhile renovating. It was dark, it was old and it didn't make full use of the existing block. In terms of bones and potential, this house was past its use-by date and definitely in need of a change.

The new building is a beauty – as wide as the block, and having a curved, timber-lined ceiling, which goes from two storeys at the front, with a decorative perforated screen on either side, to one storey in the middle, before curving up again at the rear, creating huge architectural interest.

The house is slightly raised at the rear, allowing for the bathroom to sit at just the right height so that when the client is in the bath, the water line is level with the pond outside the window. A small platform cantilevers above the pond, forming a tranquil garden oasis. In keeping with the Bali brief, another pond cascades down the side of the house next to lushly planted garden walls, which means there are views to water and greenery from every window.

The floor plan is unique. While a lot of houses on similar sized blocks in the area are two storeys and take up as much of the land as possible, this one seemed to strike a compromise, allowing some areas to expand out to the boundary while others shrank into the centre, letting light pour in on three of the four sides of the block. An internal courtyard allows light into the centre of the building too.

The house is modest, to suit the owners' agenda. They want to live quietly when they're on their own or be able to open the house up when guests are there, with an open-plan living, kitchen, dining and courtyard area. There's a gym and storeroom underneath, behind the garage, to accommodate the 'stuff' they just can't let go of. The bedrooms all have large robes and there's also ample space in the laundry, which is hidden away behind pocket doors. This lets it function as a laundry when open but not impede the hallway to the second bathroom and side entrance when the doors are closed.

Hallways tend to eat up valuable space; the architect solved this by making the study, guest bedroom and TV room interconnect. You can walk through the TV room and guest bedroom to the study. This wouldn't work if the bedroom was used every day, but for this couple it was perfect. When guests do stay, two cavity sliding doors close on either end of the bedroom to shut it off from the study and TV room. The owner can also access the study – her office – from the front courtyard.

The architect did a fantastic job before I started, but the clients called me in to create an interior that truly reflected the luxury Balinese brief.

Design elements

INSPIRATION

With this project, it wasn't difficult to be inspired. I had plenty of ideas from my travels through Bali, and luckily had bought a bunch of luxury interior books on my last trip there. Details from all over the place made their way into the design meetings I had with my clients. Books, magazines and various objects from their travels through Asia were all included for consideration. There were pieces of art, a gong and a number of keepsakes that were shown as being significant. The visual tone of the intention behind the building started to take shape.

Books were marked with stickers, and details were discussed in broad terms, allowing us to be flexible with how exactly the puzzle would piece together. We travelled to showrooms, picked up tile samples, worked through options and discussed every detail. The interesting thing about doing any project is the amount of detail you need to consider. If you look at every single element at once, it can become overwhelming. Sit down and make a list of everything – the hinges, the handles, the tiles, the floor grates, the tapware, the joinery, the finishes, the paint colours for every surface – well, you get the idea how much there is to decide on. You need to be gentle with yourself about how exactly this process is going to work for you.

BALINESE STARTING POINT

Every project has a unique starting point – it may be the clients' artwork that determines the direction of the interiors, or perhaps some furniture they love. In this case, the limestone flooring we chose very early on had a bearing on so many other elements of the design.

At the back of the property, there was a lot of sandstone that was going to be included in the house in some way, and would help give it its natural palette. However, we all thought limestone was particularly appropriate to the Balinese luxury look – it's used extensively at Alila. It is bright and crisp, but an absolute horror for anyone with kids or pets; with those practical considerations removed, we jumped at the chance to include it. We still had to think about details such as scuff marks and general wear; the clients didn't want to feel as if they'd either be walking on eggshells or having to clean constantly, which is no fun at all. We chose a limestone with some variations in it, so that any everyday bumps didn't show up on a stark white base.

The best outcomes are considered and not rushed, coherent and tie together all elements, but to protect your own mental wellbeing, balance needs to be found between thorough examination and paralysis by analysis. One of the best pieces of advice I ever received was to consider everything step by step. There always needs to be a starting point – in this case the limestone floors which were going to be used almost everywhere – and we then had to decide where to go from there. The logical next step was to work out what other tiles for other spaces would work best with the limestone. That was one nice easy step to solve. I'm not saying you isolate decisions and worry only about how one section works, but it's easier to break down the parts of your project that work immediately in relation to each other and find solutions for those, put them aside and then move onto the next chunk. I'll go into more detail of the tile selection a bit later, when we get to individual rooms.

Opposite: Small niches in the master bedhead take the place of traditional bedside tables.

Right, top: The varying levels of living and entertaining spaces add interest in the long, narrow home.

Right, below: It can be effective to partially conceal favourite pieces to add an element of surprise.

Below: Home office spaces benefit from styling – flowers, books and candles add an element of domesticity.

Opposite: In a narrow walkway space, a vertical garden acts as a screen to a neighbouring property as well as being beautiful in its own right.

Some thoughts on editing

The decision-making process relies heavily on the brief. If a finish or inclusion reflects the intention of the brief then it gets considered. If it doesn't, it gets filed away for another day. Similarly, if you fall in love with something on your sourcing journey and it doesn't look as if it will work in terms of your inspiration and visual reference, unfortunately that needs to be shelved for another day too. But sometimes those unexpected things do, in fact, manage to fit into the scheme.

The challenge is working with all these elements; the ones that are just right, the curveballs and the absolute must-haves. If something isn't working, look again, look wider, look differently, but look for an alternative solution that will fit better into the puzzle.

A great home doesn't contain only things you love, but rather, things you love that happen to work with what you're intending to achieve. This editing process, as long and sometimes frustrating as it can be, is the key to a successful result.

You can fall head over heels with something you see in a magazine or book, only to realise it doesn't work with your life after all. It takes understanding of who is in the space, what they need from it, how many times it will be used, what it needs to be maintained and so on to be sure that what you're planning to use or do makes sense. It takes understanding, too, that what you're trying to include will not just flourish but also survive everyday life in your home.

Opposite: Feature mosaic tiles create a dramatic contrast to the light-filled and otherwise very white master ensuite.

Rooms under the spotlight

I've found there's no uniform way of dealing with a project – it's not as if you start at the front of the house and work towards the back, or start with living areas and go from there. It all depends on the project and, in this one, finding that limestone early on made a huge difference as to how to proceed. It made sense to then think of all the other floor and wall tiles that would be used in the house – and that basically meant moving straight on to bathrooms.

THE BATHROOMS

The ensuite bathroom started with a mother of pearl mosaic tile we found very early on while looking for the initial limestone, and immediately became a must-have to be worked around. Because it's so flamboyant and the house was the opposite, the rest of the interior finishes of the ensuite really needed to be restrained, to be pulled back in terms of gloss level, texture and interest. In contrast to the small mosaic wall tiles which look handmade with their irregular shape, the bathroom floor tiles are large and almost painterly with their brushstroke texture.

A bathroom isn't an island. It doesn't stand alone, an oasis in the desert of the creative process, existing without consequence to the rest of the home. Its finishes need to work with other bathrooms in the home. It needs to have some dialogue and commonality with the kitchen, and it needs to work in harmony with adjoining bedrooms so it appears to belong together.

CHOOSING THE RIGHT TILE

The tile choices in the ensuite flowed into the guest bathroom. The wall and floor tiles are the same, but the feature tile from the ensuite, the mother of pearl mosaic, was replaced in the guest bathroom with something even bolder. They look a little like an oversized woven travertine basket, and add texture and amazing interest into an otherwise pulled back and restrained bathroom. The tiles aren't an everywhere tile either, not just for the fact that they're really quite bold, but also because they're a cleaning nightmare – another nod to the fact this is a home for two people and their occasional guests. If the bathroom was occupied regularly, the cleaning might just break your heart, but they're in a room that's used by friends dropping by for a glass of wine or a cup of tea, not handled by youngsters rushing to school.

The vanities in both the ensuite and the guest bathrooms are not sourced but designed, using timber veneer and Caesarstone that are a good contrast to the white-white-whiteness of the bathroom tiles, allowing for a bit of interest but in an appropriately understated and luxurious way. Stone basins with a nice thin profile and milky white matt finish complement the tiles perfectly. The rest of the design involved specifying lighting (making sure it was positioned to cast no shadows from one side or create that hollow-eyed look) and choosing taps and accessories. Face-level cabinets with power inside provide additional storage on top of that in the vanities; semi-opaque electric exterior blinds were installed, and so too

Opposite: The water level in the bath, when filled, is in line with the pond outside the window.

In the guest bathroom, the travertine tiles, difficult to clean, are used only on a feature wall.

was underfloor heating. In my opinion, though, the most interesting element of all in the bathrooms is invisible. The ceilings have been fitted with stealth speakers that sit underneath the paintwork and have been plastered over. They're positioned so that the owner can enjoy a glass of wine, some mellow tunes and a view out to the pond and luscious tropical garden.

All the bathroom decisions were made in one neat bundle, which meant that one large chunk was done. This also led to one of the main elements in the kitchen – the super white granite in the island bench which relates to the tiles in the guest bathroom.

THE OPEN-PLAN LIVING AREA AND KITCHEN

The next part of the project involved tackling the main open-plan living, dining and kitchen area. The challenge in such a space is how to demarcate the different areas. Zoning is obviously the solution and the good, predictable ways, such as pendant lighting and a giant rug, were appropriate here too. But what happens where one area meets the next? What do you do when you have one large space with two completely different functions? In this case, the kitchen sits next to the living room, and they both have a wall of built-in joinery sharing the same wall. How do you differentiate one from the other but make them play nicely together? Ah, there's the rub.

Form following function and purpose-led design were the answers in this particular scenario. The joinery unit became defined by its functions; in the living and dining areas, it is a TV unit and fireplace – albeit highly designed and beautiful, much like a TV unit on steroids. On the kitchen side, it contains three pantries and the fridge, which is integrated into a cabinet, allowing the rest of the kitchen to shine.

Right: The curve of the timber ceiling is reflected in the curve of the fireplace.

MAKING DIFFERENT ZONES

It was important for the joinery unit to function quite differently in the kitchen from the living and dining area, and yet still look like one piece. This was done by continuing the line at the top of the overhead cabinets all the way through the living and dining area into the kitchen. Giving the upper and lower panels uniformity in both spaces – with all being of the same material, finished to the same gloss level, and of the same shape and size – allows the two rooms to easily relate to each other.

There are important differences between the two spaces, though, in terms of materials. The lounge room side is warm and cosy, focused around the fire. On the other hand, the kitchen, being a workspace, required harder, cooler, more precise finishes. Where the fireplace is swathed in recycled wood, the kitchen is centred around a solid quartzite block that is an island of functionality in the middle of the space. The stone is also used on the bench either side of the cooktop.

The contrast, too, between the fireplace and kitchen designs sets the areas apart. The kitchen is monolithic, structured and linear, while the fireplace, wedged between the upper and lower cabinets, is curved and gentle. The massive TV is integrated into the timber joinery, and the fireplace is tucked in under the curve, with a concealed flue. Where the timber finishes, the kitchen starts and that change of material and the structural beam in between delineates the spaces. However, looking from the front, the two units are in essence one long line of joinery.

THE IMPORTANCE OF LIGHTING

Lighting also helps demarcate the spaces. Continuing with the curvy theme of the living area with its sweeping timber ceiling and the curving timber fireplace, the lighting overhead is a real statement. Large – in fact, oversized – pendants hang in a group of three, closely resembling something like fabric-covered shark eggs. These float below mirrored plates that reflect the light back down to the seating below.

The kitchen, too, has its own special lighting treatment, though balance had to be sought between the two adjoining spaces as the massive shark egg lights would fight with anything too gregarious. Hanging above the island bench are small, matt black teardrops that relate nicely to the matt black LED downlights dotted around the perimeter of the timber ceilings.

FLOORING

A large rug in the living room again adds to the contrast between the softness of one space and the crispness of the other. Custom made to fit under all the furniture but allowing the tiles to be a walkway from the front door, the rug is a quiet star of the space. Its subtlety and beauty are its strengths; it plays so nicely into the overall colour scheme that it can almost be glossed over as a base rather than jumping out and competing with major features such as the fireplace and overhead lighting.

Left: The kitchen stands separate from the living area through its use of white, both in the joinery and the island.

Opposite: Black downlights and simple pendants tie in with other black elements in the kitchen, including handles, appliances and chairs.

Opposite: Plum is a colour used throughout the house – in the dining area, it's found in the chairs and artwork.

The use of colour

CHOOSING THE RIGHT MIX

The colour palette of the Bondi house is simple and neutral, the epitome of a classic and contemporary scheme with its whites, off-whites, browns and greys. A neutral scheme gives the freedom to layer other colours – colour is subjective and I think about it in the same way I think about music. One person likes opera and another likes pop – neither is wrong; they both love what they love and perceive their love through rose-coloured glasses.

The main bedroom has a subtle accent of plum and gold with the sheer drapery containing various lively shades of both. The plum colour comes through in the dressing chair in the corner of the room. The key when using colour, or any decorating element really, is to use some for dramatic effect and then tie that back into the room elsewhere, in a different way, in a different amount. That can mean something as literal as plum chair and plum drapes, but can also mean something as subtle as a copper metallic, a blush fabric and a soft pink flower. All three elements have the same basic colour and hue, but are made of different materials that feel different and have different light-reflecting qualities.

Pinks actually make their way into the home in a few areas. The TV room rug, for example, mixes soft pastel pink with purple, grey and mustardy-goldy yellow. These colours make their way onto the sofa in the form of feather-filled cushions, and even book spines and covers pick up the slightest hint of the accent colour.

Because the client loved the plum of the drapery so much, we decided that the dining room chairs would be plum, as would be the artwork for that area. The same tones are picked up elsewhere in the home in plants, orchids and kangaroo paw flowers, with that hint and repeat being the key to making the colour fit well in the home. It's like warming up your eyes to expect what they're about to see. The plum comes as less and less of a shock the more you see it in small amounts in varied places.

USING A PALETTE OF COLOURS

It's important not to choose just one colour, though; that would be boring. It comes back to the previous statement about colour coming as less of a shock, as there are good and bad shocks when it comes to decorating. You want the good shock or, more aptly, the surprise, to enliven your responses. When you keep seeing the same thing, it becomes as boring as being served the same breakfast, lunch and dinner week in, week out. Even the best meal will become humdrum, and the same is true for colour.

Using a palette of colours is absolutely the way to go, making sure the ones you use belong in the same range. To guarantee this, look at the basic principles of colour, and take notice of complement and contrast. Complementary colours have the most contrast and are opposites on the colour wheel, plum and gold being one example. You're guaranteed a harmonious result if you use complementary colours. There are also analogous palettes, meaning three or four colours immediately adjacent on the colour wheel, such as yellow, lime and green, or red, orange and yellow. These combos complement each other and work well together, too.

The basket-like light fitting adds to the resort vibe of the house.

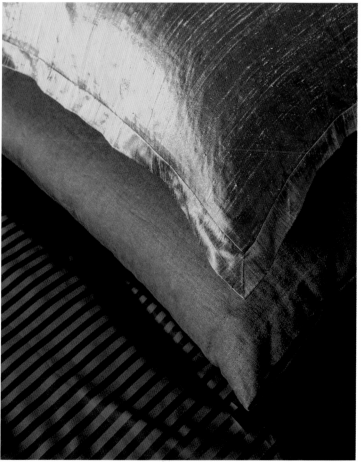

In practice, in the Bondi home, this palette is a blend of complementary colours – plum and gold – and analogous, coming through in the blues and purples that appear elsewhere in other rooms. Four colours next to each other on the colour wheel are blue, purple, indigo and red and these are the four accent colours we used. Without the knowledge that an analogous colour scheme works well, you might think that red and plum can never coexist in the same palette, but the result proves otherwise. A red console in one room, plum dining area in another, plus blue art and gold accents add up to a layered and varied palette, not sticking with one safe colour accent, but still abiding by the general colour rules.

Using a palette of colours is absolutely the way to go – just be sure to use those that belong in the same range.

Above: Plum accents in the master bedroom can be found in the chair upholstery as well as the subtle gold to plum tones of the sheer curtains.

Left: A slubby gold silk that was chosen by the client to reflect her love of Thai culture, brings a sense of vibrant luxury to the master bedroom.

Opposite: The framed tribal necklace, against a background of charcoal textured wallpaper, gives a luxurious edge to the television room.

Adding an extra layer

LIMITING MATERIALS

Paring back was really the challenge in this project. The materials palette was taking shape, and consisted of limestone; matt, milky white tiles; a little bit of glamour here and there in terms of stone or timber or mother of pearl, and an emerging pop of contrasting black (see page 29). The palette could have become too busy if we didn't start to limit any future materials, colours or textures. The key with any coherent palette is consistency in terms of colours, materials and textures, while striking a balance with contrasting elements.

A great example of this is in the use of western red cedar (see page 37). The curved ceiling was always such a massive feature that the choice of colour and timber type was crucial. We had to balance that against budget and availability of timber options for doors and windows. We narrowed down the selection of appropriate timbers for the many openings as any staining, special timbers or special treatments would have eaten up large chunks of the budget. Every little bit counts, and this is one of those decisions you need to consider closely; finishes and inclusions that vary by $10 or $20 per item can blow your budget when the number of items, or area of use, is large.

It's the same with tiles, which are a major feature at this house, going from literally the front gate to the rear courtyard, while leapfrogging the main bedroom. That's a lot of tiles; to cut down on costs, we had to find something that would be less expensive than the limestone, but work well with it, be hard-wearing and not show up every mark. There also needed to be an internal and outdoor rated

finish in the same size and exact type of limestone, which made the parameters of our search shrink to a more manageable chunk. The clearer you are in your requirements, your brief, your style and your constraints, the easier it is to brief the salespeople helping you to flesh out your vision, allowing them to show you four choices instead of forty.

BEING CAREFUL WITH CHOICES

The wall tiles, for instance, were very expensive but, because the bathrooms aren't huge, our exposure to a blow-out was kept under control. The floor tiles in the bathrooms were cheaper, although still appropriate for a luxury home but, again, the areas covered were limited, containing our exposure even further. The feature tiles, which in essence were only on one wall of each bathroom were where the money was spent, as we figured that for each wall we required only around six square metres, so we could afford to be a little more indulgent. The result of this indulgence is clear; the feature wall in each bathroom is the major drawcard and money definitely well spent.

WALL FINISHES AND FABRICS

Other well-considered and well-delivered luxury expenses for this adult family home are in the wall finishes. Aside from the palette being so simple, or perhaps because of it, we decided to add an extra background layer to almost

every room by treating some of the walls with wallpaper. The guest bedroom has a lovely champagne-coloured vinyl wall covering (see page 41) that looks, for all intents and purposes, like a lovely slubby silk but without the maintenance issues. The TV room has two types of grasscloth paper, a dark charcoal and a bronze, each with a different texture and pattern, adding to that Balinese luxury appeal. These finishes are fussy in a way, and not particularly hard-wearing, but are perfect for this room, one of the most adult of the adult spaces. It's a grown-up room with a grown-up aesthetic, dark and sultry, functional but very comfy, built for two to lounge around in, watching their favourite film.

The living room also has a vinyl wall covering, the same type and brand as used in the guest bedroom but in a soft off-white to complement the colour scheme of both that room and the house overall. The dining room has a much more dramatic wall covering that looks like thin paperbark sitting in front of silver leaf (see page 31). Hints and glints of the silver flicker through gaps and cracks in the matt bronze paper-textured finish.

An interesting thing about the dining room is that the wallpapered wall is the only wall to speak of. The opposite wall is made up of glass doors opening onto the courtyard, and the two walls to the left and right are mainly windows, meaning they only needed an appropriate window dressing to give them a little more substance.

The fabric in this room, which was chosen to work with the wallpaper, is actually the result of one of those rare, synergistic, client/designer collaboration moments. I had asked my client to meet me at a showroom in Sydney to show her one particular fabric. It was something I knew was right for this room and I had my heart set on it.

We wandered around the showroom while I tried to locate the particular sample I had seen several months earlier. Without prompting, she managed to find it. It's a real buzz when client and designer have an affinity and shared aesthetic that makes the design process as close to painless as possible.

THE IMPORTANCE OF AN OVERVIEW

All interior elements have to work in harmony, but you can't possibly know all at once what those elements will be. It is important to piece together the puzzle using your brief and reference as a guide, but also allowing your desires, your preferences and your gut to lead you.

To ensure that all elements will work together, don't start spending straightaway, but pencil in where each thing might go. It's only by finding pieces, gathering samples or having images of all inclusions and then seeing them together as an overview of the whole scheme that you can be sure that you've got it right. When you have, that's when you order, you buy, you let your credit card out from its hiding place to wreak havoc on your budget.

Left: Prized pieces from the owners' travels have found landing spaces within the home.

Opposite: Layered with textures inside and out, the exterior is clad in western red cedar, the same material used for windows and the living room ceiling.

Focal points

CREATING DRAMA

When you're dealing with a scheme as simple as cedar and stone, you need to look for opportunities to add some drama – to create focal points in each room to elevate their appeal from what could be seen as safe and conservative to something that elicits a response, a remark and a feeling.

While the lighting described earlier helps demarcate the living room space, the wall of joinery containing the fireplace and television is the true hero of the room. A curved plane bends gently around the fireplace flue while a flat plane surrounds the TV and works its way behind the fire. Storage forms part of the structure of the wall, and the reclaimed timber pieces work really well with the rustic yet refined nature of a luxury Balinese resort brief.

The adjoining kitchen also has a focal point that's equally structural. The island bench, or more particularly the stone it's made of, is a massive standout. Known as super white granite, it is a lovely soft and veined stone that looks a little like a grey marble while being harder and more durable. The veins in the stone are reminiscent of the branches on a tree and the monolithic scale and form of the island bench really makes a solid statement.

The dining room's focal point is the lighting, though in such a simple space the wallpaper comes a very close second. There isn't anything wrong with having several bold elements in a room as long as their drama is noticed in a hierarchical manner – by which I mean the most dramatic feature stands out first, then you notice the next and the next and so on. By staggering this dramatic impact you allow objects to sit comfortably with each other, rather

Below: This home is not short on drama; it's hard to decide whether the curved fireplace or the oversized fabric lights are more of a focal point.

than fighting for attention. If you have a whole bunch of elements in a room that are equally vibrant or interesting, there's the risk that it will be overwhelming.

The master bedroom has several features, from the drop-down television screen to the dressing chair, but the first thing you notice is the bedhead (see page 18). Wrapped in bronze crumpled vinyl, it is the centre of the room and the main visual element of the space. The black Asian screened wardrobe doors are pretty great too, but they mostly fade into the background and hide the transition from bedroom to ensuite, which is all about the feature tile, the mother of pearl mosaic mentioned earlier. The other bathroom's focal point is the bumpy travertine.

TV rooms are all about viewing, but the rug has to be the focal point in the space, allowing everything else to be simple and relatively monochromatic, and giving the room a fun and colourful base on which to sit.

The art is the focal point in the guest bedroom (see opposite), and the study has amazing Thai temple doors that lead out onto the front terrace. Each space has its own centrepiece, some being more bold and eye-catching than others. It's important to realise that rooms don't all need big bold statements; the statements need to suit the function of each room, the size of the space and the level of use that they receive.

Left: Thai temple doors, with oxidised metal hardware, lead into the study space.

Opposite: Subtle layering can help create focal points – here, a champagne-coloured drape and silk-look wall covering allow the blues of the bedcover and artwork to stand out.

DECORATION

The building was beautifully designed and the brief was almost freedom personified; if the project ended at the point at which the walls were painted or papered and the furniture installed, the house would be a sight to behold, yet something would be missing.

As a reality TV contestant, I learnt a valuable lesson in styling. I was focused purely on the building and layout, looking mostly at lighting and flow. Furniture was a secondary consideration and decoration was a very, *very* distant third. I didn't understand the value of telling a story with décor – showing who lives in the space, how they live and what they love. Thankfully, though, I was able to see, through other contestants' work, that a well-styled space, and well-styled home, has a certain finished quality to it.

The North Bondi home had beautiful art, great form, flow and furniture, but it was through layering in large format photographic books, plants and décor items that the spaces felt the way a home should feel. No one, or at least no one fun, lives in a photoshoot 24/7. There's no joy in sterility, and it's the quirky things from your travels that paint a picture of where you've been and who you are.

You have to blend these found items into the space. Some may work perfectly with your brand new home, and others may simply be too sentimentally significant to hide away or let go of. The owners had accumulated some pieces over many years of travelling, and these have been integrated with some new-for-the-home but nevertheless rustic and Oriental new purchases.

The new Thai dancing lady statues take pride of place on one of the consoles next to a treasured gong the owners have loved for years. The coffee tables are dressed with a blend of old and new books and décor, while the bookshelf in the island bench simply requires the books to be arranged to create some interest through variation of height and shape.

It's the blend of old and new that elevates a home. Creating the sweet spot is a matter of both honouring the things you love and bringing in pieces that are appropriate to the brief, and that help set the style and mood you are aiming for.

My go-tos for decoration are books, lamps, décor items, candles and plants. As much as I know these bring a space to life, there's still the concern that the particular items I've found won't be the life givers I intend them to be. I source any number of pieces that feel like I want the home to feel, that have the style that the owner is wanting to achieve, and that work with a simple colour and material palette. I hope on hope that when they arrive and are ready to be layered in, they will do the project justice. I find a spot for each appropriate piece and get reminded by the happy clients, my team and even myself that the décor I thought should work actually works beautifully.

Creating the sweet spot is a matter of both honouring the things you love and bringing in pieces that are appropriate to the brief.

Left: With the addition of artefacts and attention to how books are arranged, bookshelves can be beautiful as well as hard-working.

Right: A fusion of old and new, the Asian console was bought new as the perfect spot for the clients' prized gong.

Below: Mirrors are a great way of adding visual depth and textured interest.

The indoor-outdoor boundary is once again blurred in an internal courtyard. All weather entertaining is possible thanks to a Vergola cover.

Pieces of
the puzzle

——

SMALL CHANGE

One room, two sofas, one coffee table, four different looks. Way back at the beginning of my career I was given the opportunity to compete on a reality TV show that pitted designers with a few years' experience against each other in a renovation competition.

I had a few years' experience and was a designer, but really didn't have much of a clue when it came to decorating – like really not much of a clue at all. I thought decorating was superfluous, and that real design was structural and based in problem solving, increasing amenity and creating greater use. But this was a renovation show, and decorating was important – I had no confidence that I could do it.

I made a call to my mentor and friend, Dayne, and asked him if he could give me a crash course. He opened his home to me and gave me a simple exercise to flex my décor muscles and give me some confidence that I had what it takes to be a designer and decorator.

Even today, I find the exercise really interesting. Dayne pulled every decorative element out of his lounge room and left only the two sofas and the coffee table. There was no art, cushions, flowers etc – just a furnished but blank space.

He then gave me a brief, describing the person who lived there and directing me to choose décor and soft furnishings that reflected each pretend person to fulfil their pretend brief. I loved the process so much I thought I'd share it with you – so here are four different takes on one simple room answering four separate briefs.

Masculine

This look is all about simplicity and layers, but keeping things comfortable and low fuss. When I think of a space built for a man to live in, I automatically think of materials such as leather, wood and metal, and raw, somewhat basic finishes.

Soft furnishings are kept to a comfortable minimum, colours being used sparingly to add interest but not huge amounts of drama. Contrast comes in the form of the shapes and textures used in the rug and the pattern of the sidetables, with large scale, concrete-look lamps being good anchors for the strong, masculine look.

As far as the palette goes, there's grey, tan leather, blue, charcoal and warm gold. The timber of the coffee table and sidetables is similar in colour to the mirror, which also reflects the colour of the tan leather. This, then, really only counts as one colour – tan or aged gold – but it is seen in three different textures and materials. The colour palette is pure and simple, which works well with the low-fuss style of a masculine décor style.

The rug is a huge impact piece but, again, it's been dialled back so it fits into the subtle colour scheme. It has plenty of pattern and visual texture, and the aged blue makes the perfect base from which to build the room, but it's not an overwhelming statement.

The back cushions on the couch have been given a little contrast by introducing a lighter grey and a navy and gold cushion. These are all the same size so as to keep consistency but add visual interest.

Tips for making a masculine room work are:

- Use a simple colour and materials palette
- Play with materials such as timber, leather, stone and metal
- Don't overdecorate
- Add living elements that are strong but simple in appearance, such as cactus, succulents and ferns, or flowers with more architectural forms
- As usual, accessorise with candles, books and *objets d'art*, but choose ones that would be appropriate for the man using the space

Feminine

This feminine look may be playing to gender stereotypes and, of course, there are any number of women who would like this or hate its uber-pink prettiness. The exercise is to demonstrate how diametrically different you can make a room look with the change of artwork, soft furnishings, décor, flowers and occasional furniture.

Firstly, the scale of the occasional furniture has been changed; the sidetables and lamps are about 80 per cent smaller than in the masculine look. This makes the sofa and coffee table look larger and the room cosier.

The artwork also has a feminine look, with the pinks and purples working in with the pastel colour scheme. The two artworks fill the wall just as well as the mirror in the masculine look; the idea is that, if placed above a sofa, whatever is on the walls should be contained within the width of the sofa with approximately 100 mm on either side from the edge of the frame to the edge of the sofa arm. This pair of artworks are the right size for the space and for the sofa. One of these pictures, as lovely as they are, would not be enough for this particular wall.

The rug is again the base from which to build the room – here, it's bright and ambient in pattern. Various coloured or neutral rugs could have worked, but this bold statement is a great way of showing how different a room can be by changing a few key inclusions.

The cushions are all linen to match the linen sofa, and in two sizes and colours – a lumbar size darker pink and a square, 50 by 50 cm light pink. They skate the line between colour coordination and matchy-matchy. I think it's on the right side of that line, but it's a close call.

Pinks are also found in the metallics used for interest in this scheme; where gold was used in the masculine scheme, here we have copper. A copper bowl adds height and interest to the coffee table, and ties in with both the round, mirrored tray sitting under the floral arrangement and the mirrored sidetables. The mirrored tray also reflects the colour of the flowers and gives a pool-like sense of depth to the coffee table.

Bright red natives light up the room and tie in with the artworks. Again, there's a fine line between matching every element in the room and being informed by elements to create a scheme, but I think it works. In terms of showing off a different look using the same basic inclusions, I think we've nailed the brief.

Tips for creating a feminine space:

- Use colours that feel feminine to you
- Flowers and colours can be bolder and brighter
- Mirror, copper and marble all fit this look
- Décor can be a little more layered and soft
- Use more delicately scaled occasional furniture

Beachy

This look is all about visual relief, nothing too gregarious and everything blending gently for a relaxed feeling.

The palette is a simple blend of white linen, bleached wood and simple textures such as wood grain or basket weaves. There's stone for textural contrast but it's in the same colour as the sofa, which reduces the stone's visual impact.

Texturally, the palette is basic, with woven elements in the form of the baskets, the tray and the silver and white cushions. Timber log textured lamps are in the same warm silver colour as the bleached oak sidetables; wool and coral flesh out the simple scheme which has been designed for minimal contrast but with enough interest to make the room work.

It's the pattern on the rug that adds interest; the grey and white are very close in depth and colour, therefore dialling back the contrast level in this space.

Even though it contains quite a lot of white, this would make a suitable family scheme. The grey linen couch covers are removable, as are the white linen cushion covers, so the occasional mishap can be easily rectified. Storage baskets sit inside the sidetables, allowing for toys or books to be easily swept out of sight when the occasion requires, and the white, hinge-topped box gives a permanent place for toys to live. This box also works equally well to store blankets or any other everyday items you need but don't want to see, and also makes good overflow guest seating.

The low maintenance and easily kept dried baby's-breath floral arrangement works in well with the no-fuss idea of the coastal living brief – it never needs to be replaced or renewed. This kind of dried flower is useful if you're styling your home to sell and don't want to constantly update flowers, though be careful as some dried flowers do look lifeless.

Tips to re-create a beach look:

- Grey, white and bleached wood work as a base
- Dial back colour to a bare minimum
- Use nautical elements such as oars, coral and driftwood, although starfish and dolphin motifs might take you in a less stylish direction
- Textures of timber, linen, wool and open basket weaves work well
- The smallest amount of black will prevent an otherwise monochromatic scheme from looking too bland
- For a low fuss and low maintenance approach to decoration, use removable covers and washable fabrics on furniture, and integrate storage into the occasional furniture

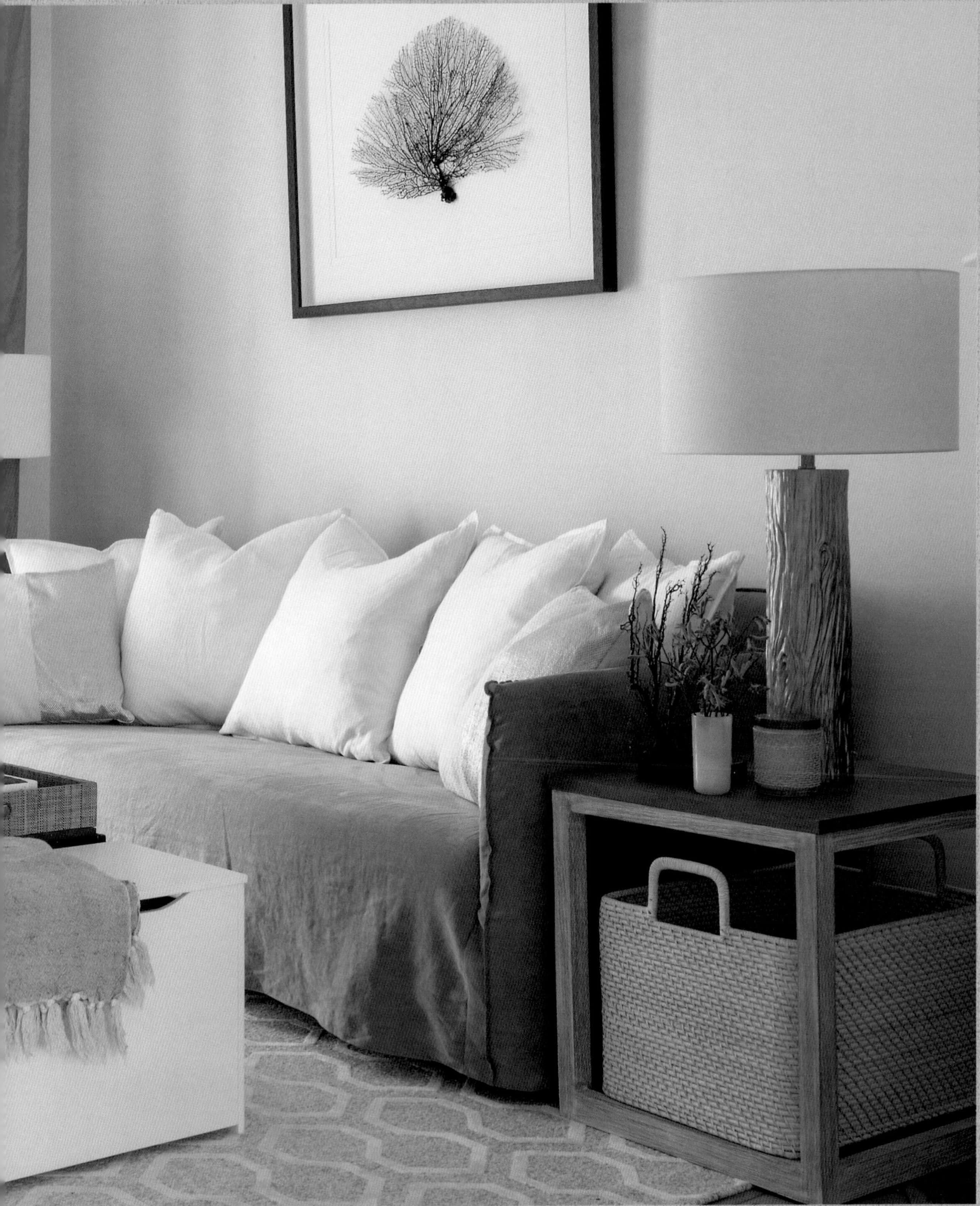

Opulent

High contrast and understated glamour is the brief of this look, with gold and blue adding a big pop of colour to the grey and white room. There's a feminine bent to it, but elements would appeal to both men and women, making it also suitable for a couple.

There's contrast and colour in every inclusion – the blue dip-dyed drapes, for instance, work perfectly to lift the room. Blues occur in floral form, in the cushions as well as the huge hydrangea arrangement, and visual interest occurs in both the ombré effect of the baskets under the coffee table and the geometric pattern in the oversized sidetables. Elegance and glamour are seen in the lustre of the gold lamps, while the mustard in the cushions works in nicely with the mirror above.

Interestingly, the rug is one of the more sedate elements in the space – anywhere else it would seem quite bold with its blue and gold ambient look, but in this instance it's simply a gentle, colourful base.

Gold décor items, succulents and scented candles and diffusers finish off this sweet looking and fragrant space.

Tips for an opulent space:

- Choose a high contrast colour scheme
- Play with your patterns – in this instance florals, but geometrics or any number of graphic looks may do the trick
- Look for high contrast in occasional furniture, such as the geometric shapes in these sidetables
- Décor can have a little more bling

It may be the case that some of these rooms work better than others, but this just shows that you can create any number of looks with little more than a new rug, a change of occasional furniture, new lamps, soft furnishings and décor.

The sofas and coffee table are the big ticket expenses of your space, so by choosing those wisely and working with a simple, neutral palette to start with, you can create rooms that change with the seasons, with the introduction of a new beau (or the exit of an old one), the addition of new family members or just the desire to give your home a new lease of life.

All it takes is a brief, an idea of the style you want to create, and some good shopping which, after all, is surely one of the best parts of decorating.

Pieces of the puzzle

Heritage apartment

BAYSIDE BOLTHOLE MAKEOVER

The brief

This Elizabeth Bay apartment in Sydney is clearly a gem. When I visited for the first time, I could see it was a little past its prime but it was a gem nonetheless. The block is a Spanish Mission style structure, with only two apartments, each the size of a family house, on each floor. The location is fantastic, perched above Rushcutters Bay Park, with views across the park and yacht masts to Sydney Harbour.

The owners have lived here comfortably for years and are about as easy to get along with as any clients I've ever had, unflappable and generally so busy with their lives that the small things simply don't matter so much. She operates her business – one of the most impressive I've come across – out of the front bedroom, while he uses the apartment purely as a home. They like to get away to their weekender as often as possible during the year.

By their own admission, though, the old girl needed a little bit of love. A facelift. A little work done. She hadn't felt a designer's touch for a good few decades. However, the owners were very clear that no walls were to be moved as the apartment functioned exactly the way they needed it to. The task at hand was simply just to solve the design problems internally and give the home a new lease of life.

It was actually the idea of renovating the kitchen that was the start of the project, because it wasn't working very well in terms of flow, aesthetic, storage or preparation areas. That turned out to be my introduction to the clients and the home.

THE HOME AS A GAUGE

The home a person chooses is more often than not a reflection of who that person is. When you're starting out, your choice is largely dictated by what you can afford but still reflects your values and lifestyle, even if you do have to make compromises. As you gain knowledge and experience and financial stability, your options usually increase. When you're able to make a choice that is based on what you really want rather than what you have to have, the home you occupy tends to fit you even better. It's a bit like a hermit crab crowbarring itself out of its old shell so it can occupy the bigger one someone has left behind. It's the circle of real estate life.

I can gauge a lot about a person from the home they have chosen. I can also tell a lot about what the home should become based on the person who owns it. It's a really neat bit of intuition that serves me well and allows me to create homes that suit different people, never repeating the same look from home to home to home.

Opposite: The fireplace, previously unusable, is now the central element of the lounge room.

Structure

POTENTIAL OF THE EXISTING HOME

The building itself is full of merit, with its high ceilings, ornate plasterwork and elegant parquetry floors. Well, that's in the building's foyer, anyway. Behind the front door of my clients' apartment, things weren't quite as grand – on the surface, at least.

I could tell, though, there was loads of potential all the way through. The apartment is essentially made up of two halves, with bedrooms and bathrooms on one side, and kitchen, living and dining rooms on the other.

The kitchen, which was the main room they wanted me to consider, is long and narrow and also had potential written all over it. However, it was a bit messy, made up of two smaller rooms with a doorway near the centre. It had three doors leading into it and two windows. In other words, it had very few walls. It's also a transitional space to what would most probably have once been the maid's quarters, but now is the front bedroom/home office. Suffice to say, there were challenges upon challenges.

The office is a workspace, so didn't need much love, and the second bedroom and TV room simply needed a little upgrade. The master bedroom wasn't quite working as well as it could be – the main thing it needed was for the bed to be centrally located and angled towards the view.

Lounge, dining and sitting rooms were all blank slates – there were any number of ways to improve them, just by thinking how they would be used, and what could be done to improve the liveability of each one.

The first thing I noticed when I walked into the lounge room was that it appeared to not get much use. There was a fireplace with no actual fireplace in it, no TV and, while the audiovisual equipment was pretty prominent, the client explained that it was rarely used. The furniture lingered awkwardly around the space, the individual pieces not really getting on together and creating a less than comfortable environment.

I asked one of the clients how she used the lounge room, and was unsurprised by her reply. 'I get a massage in here once a week.' Yep. This is the room with amazing harbour views. It's the room with a big central fireplace and ornate cornices. It's the room with honey-coloured, thin parquetry floors and generous period skirtings and architraves. And that's without mentioning the archway and the balcony with a view, and the connection to the dining room in one long glorious hall. Something had to be done.

Opposite: A water-based flooring product brings back the natural colour of the timber.

ARCHITECTURAL INTEREST

Buildings like this one are chock full of architecturally beautiful elements, the sort of things you don't see included in developments anymore. The windows are ornate, with colonial bars running through them to give an elegant 'grid' style which looks perfectly quaint. All the internal doors are panelled and the door handles so beautifully worn that it would have been a crime to replace them. The fireplace in the lounge room, one of the most perfect architectural centrepieces in any home, is dark green marble that needed only a bit of attention to come back to life. There are ornate details, not just in the cornices but also in the air vents above the windows, the archway into the sleeping part of the home and even the sweet dado rails running around the perimeter of the living areas.

The main bathroom had plenty of heritage merit as well. The bath, basin and tiles, while all a bit tired, were pretty darn beautiful. Marble, chrome and elegant, they are just the things you would want to install in a home like this.

It's an absolute crime to tamper with elements such as these; it's best to honour them, even if you decide you want to modernise the space. In the '70s and '80s, so many of these beautiful buildings were stripped of their heritage pieces in favour of the brutal hard lines favoured at the time. It's a sad thing to see, so whenever you are working with a home with heritage interest and so much architectural detail perfectly intact, it's your duty to bring it back to its former glory. That's not to say the apartment was perfect – there was definitely room for improvement.

THE LAYOUT

As mentioned, one side of this apartment is made up of bedrooms and bathrooms; the other half consists of kitchen, living and dining rooms.

In multi-residential buildings, as is the case here, there is almost always a repeated floor plan. It is interesting how things change over time, and how different apartments evolve, as new owners move in and make their mark. In this building, some of the neighbours had changed the original layout quite a lot. In one apartment, for instance, the kitchen had been made into a walkway/library and the new kitchen was in an entirely different spot. Seeing some of the ways neighbours had dealt with their floor plans made us think about different solutions for this apartment.

Below: The sofa, reupholstered in grey velvet, was the only piece of existing furniture to make it through the cull.

Some thoughts
on floor plans

When I first started my career, my big dream was to buy an apartment to renovate. With the Sydney property market being what it was, I didn't think I'd ever be able to get there. The solution was to join forces with three friends and make the plunge into property together.

The apartment we bought was next door to that of a good friend, with whom we shared a wall. The two apartments were identical in floor plan, with exceptions. Over the building's 70-year life span, walls and doorways had been changed to suit various owners' lifestyles.

Where we had a kitchen, next door had a dressing room; where they had a kitchen, we had a lounge room. It's a really interesting thing to think about the organic and responsive nature of a building and how it morphs and evolves to suit its owners and occupants.

It's wise to ask your neighbours, or at least look online to see how other apartments' floor plans may have changed over the years to assess what layout will work best for you. By doing this simple bit of research, you can find solutions you may not have thought of, or solve problems you didn't even know you had. It will also save you lots of paper – that might otherwise have been screwed up – featuring version after version of floor plan changes that didn't quite work. If you're working with a designer, it may also mean making plenty of savings, as you'll be clearer about the potential layout before you engage them. Don't forget to speak to your body corporate or company title board of directors, too – some buildings are stricter than others about exactly what you can do inside your apartment.

Below: Panelled doors, colonial bar windows and ornate vents provide the heritage details.

Opposite: Soft pastel green, pink and lilac work to create a restful bedroom palette.

Below: The colour scheme ties in with the existing window treatments and window seat upholstery.

Because the window coverings were so good, I worked with them as the starting point.

NATURAL LIGHT

Sometimes in these beautiful old buildings, the light levels can be a challenge. In a previous period apartment I've owned, there were only four windows in the whole place. On top of that, buildings are often hemmed in on each side, which means the light either comes in from the façade or through tiny windows in alleyways at the back.

That wasn't the case in this apartment, which had light for days. It had windows in every single room, with three of the four boundary walls being external ones and the fourth shared with a common hallway. The rooms were so flooded with light the main challenge was how to manage it. This had been such a major issue, in fact, that the owners had solved it on their own not long before I had first come to look at the job. They'd had custom blinds, of elegant patterns and colours, made for each bedroom – I didn't have to think about that task. Because the window coverings were so good, I worked with them as the starting point and we chose colours to suit in each space. The living spaces had no privacy issues – they weren't overlooked at all. The kitchen, which could be seen from other buildings, had original textured glass windows for privacy.

In homes like this, where light is bright and there is no issue with trying to liven up the place, you are blessed with the choice to use any colour that lights your fire.

Opposite: The colonial bars are replicated in the fluted glass floor-to-ceiling cabinet at one end of the kitchen.

Design elements

INSPIRATION

The start of the project was really based around functional, almost utilitarian, improvement works. The clients are practical, and the home needed to be practical, too. At the same time, I still needed to be aware of the aesthetic requirement. For me, that meant creating an interior that worked with the heritage of the building, not emphasising Spanish Mission so much, but rather being inspired by certain elements such as the parquetry and the colonial bars on the windows. That felt like a sensible place to begin.

Interestingly, too, the kitchen provided a useful starting point. Given it wasn't at its best, it was safe to assume the clients saw their fair share of restaurants – and one in particular was mentioned as a reference point. The colonial bars are used there, too, as well as brass, fluted glass and marble with elements of timber and a modern take on the traditional. With that one reference handed to me by the client, the aesthetic brief was communicated clearly. I knew exactly what to do, at least in the kitchen.

Working from a single idea is great. Working from many images is also fine, but when you're looking for inspiration, the most important thing is to get a clear, almost narrow view of what you are trying to achieve and then work towards it. That means that anything outside your view should be shelved for another project another day. The clearer your visual communication of the brief is, the easier your problem solving will be.

SOURCING

The project was created in stages, the first part being the kitchen, the next the bathroom, the next being the rest of the home, so sourcing for the whole home was actually broken up into more manageable sections over the period of a year. However, when sourcing for one particular space, most choices were locked away all at once, with the brief, the creative direction and the client in mind at all times.

With the colonial bars, parquetry and a lovely palette in mind, much of the inspiration came from visits to showrooms to look for things that might work within the classic style we had settled on. Some amazing encaustic tiles I'd seen a while before in my design travels sprang to mind for use in the kitchen. Doing my job well has a lot to do with how much I notice; when I'm sourcing things for a project, I'm always keeping an eye open for other beautiful and interesting things. It might be a tile or a piece of fabric or any number of pieces of the puzzle; and, when the right time comes, these elements will bubble up to the surface. The encaustic tiles belonged to that category – something I'd loved from afar, and filed away wondering when the day might come that I'd get to use them.

Sourcing for the bathroom was relatively easy, as it was mainly a case of looking for lights. We found a beautiful wall sconce made from aged brass, as well as some simple and contemporary LED downlights.

THE KITCHEN COMPONENTS

As you should know by now, there's no wisdom in loving a certain product, locking it in and then designing the rest of the home hoping it will all work out. Ideally, you have to fill in all the details so you can make good decisions where all your choices work in harmony.

In a kitchen, for instance, that process can be pretty simple, especially in a white one. The elements you have to think about are benchtop, underbench cupboard front, overhead cupboard front, splashback, tapware, sink, appliances, storage and hardware solutions and handles.

For a long time I was loath to use handles in a kitchen. I thought they were clumsy and basic, taking away from the sculptural nature of the room. Time passes, new ideas emerge and my aesthetic has become more detailed, and handles have become something of a love of mine. There are so many fantastic options, including handmade, interestingly shaped, traditional and contemporary, that I now think of them as serving the same role as earrings do to a beautiful face. They can be drab or they can be a statement in themselves, elevating the basic fronts to something more appealing.

Handles in this project were sourced online, from the website Overstock.com. The type is appropriate for a Shaker-style kitchen but the finish gives a contemporary twist. Aged brass handles tied in beautifully with the charcoal in the floor tile and, along with the Shaker-style cupboard fronts, the scheme now had three elements.

White can be a bit too safe, but it is also the most popular kitchen colour in terms of sales. The trick to a white kitchen is to add in interest and contrast. Being so heavily patterned, the tile does just that.

Benchtops can be difficult to source. I have only ever used natural stone once. The reason for this is really dull – it's liability. Stone suppliers don't guarantee the stone once it's installed. If it marks, it marks. That's kind of tough, as porosity is a given with natural stone. Some stones are also softer or more brittle than others, so you can get chipping, and most stones will react to anything acidic like tomato sauce, lemon juice or red wine. If they come in contact with the stone – and they always do – you end up with duller, less reflective areas, and the overall effect won't be uniform. Whenever I have disclosed this information to a client, every single time, bar one, they have decided they didn't want the responsibility of such a material, and I don't blame them one bit.

This kitchen, though, would have been so lovely with marble benchtops – they seriously would look the business with their soft, natural veining. The next best thing was a composite reproduction of natural stone. There are ever more options on the market replicating marble veining, and the one I used in this project is a really nice example. Soft, grey and white and, like my clients, the perfect compromise between practicality and aesthetic.

My clients helped a lot with the appliance specification as they really had their hearts set on a freestanding cooktop, but with an induction top. That was a really easy fix because there aren't that many on the market. Quality was more appealing than price, and that narrowed the choice down to one. Teaming the modern look of the classic freestanding cooker with an ultra modern and technologically advanced rangehood that was as much a design as a functional piece was the perfect solution.

I'm a strong advocate of integrated appliances, especially when you are trying to achieve a pure look, like that of a Shaker style. Shaker style is about utility first but also about being absolutely unadorned and honest in design. It may have been developed nearly 250 years ago by an American religious group, but it fits incredibly well into the homes of today.

The tapware, too, had that nod to classic but with a modern functionality. A hand-held pull-out spray is brilliantly functional, and a classic tap is what the kitchen was absolutely begging for. We found a tap that did both, and Robert's your mother's brother, specification for the kitchen was done.

Opposite: Classic, if not heritage, details abound in the kitchen and include brass cup handles, a Shaker door profile, fluted glass and subway tiles.

Rooms under the spotlight

I've already dealt with sourcing design elements for the kitchen on page 71 – that often happens very early on a job. Now let's have a look at some of the structural challenges we faced with this renovation.

THE KITCHEN

The kitchen layout was a mess, so that needed sorting out. As well as ripping out the fittings and starting again, we put cabinets into previously unused or tight spaces to make it work as a room rather than as a transitional area.

Designing the new kitchen and getting approval for it was done ahead of time, but the removal and replacement of the cabinets happened while my clients were away on a two-week holiday. It took far less time than the usual kitchen renovation, but in special circumstances I'm able to get my suppliers to achieve the impossible.

STORAGE, BENCHTOPS AND TILING

Storage was built along a tricky wall adjoining the study. This part of the room was too shallow to accommodate the benchtop that was there before, cutting across the study doorway. The solution was to create a wall of 300 mm–deep cabinets to store glasses, crockery and the odd bottle of wine. The cabinet doors, of fluted glass panels with dark charcoal frames, give the room that lovely classical appeal while adding a nice tall, dark wall which serves as the perfect backdrop.

As soon as the cabinets were installed, the benchtops were check measured and the manufacturing started. Then came the tiling from bench to ceiling while the plumber and electrician installed the oven and other appliances.

My clients arrived home to their new kitchen, full of new storage solutions, in the middle of the night after a long flight. It must have been quite a shock, even though they were expecting it to be done while they were away.

KITCHEN FLOW

There were plenty of surprises in the new kitchen – planned surprises, but surprises for the client nonetheless. The kitchen flows seamlessly from function to function. The pantry and fridge are located between the doorway from the dining room and the doorway dividing the two sections of the kitchen. It has become a kind of food storage alcove with a little bench section opposite where you can drop off groceries before stashing them away in the pantry. The fridge is concealed behind cabinet doors. Drawers in the custom-made pantry work beautifully, and the cabinet doors of the pantry and fridge match the side panel of the newly created cupboard in the other section of the kitchen. This cupboard is in a previously unusable corner, and creates much-needed extra storage. The old layout had overhead cupboards above the cooktop, while in the new layout these have been done away with in order to make the long narrow room look not quite so narrow.

MAKING ROOM FOR EVERYTHING

When planning a new kitchen, plot out your existing kitchen to see how much space you have for the various functions and for storage. That way, you can be sure of creating more than enough space for everything. It's as simple as measuring out the drawer or cupboard sizes for each item, such as plastic containers, plates and bowls, glasses and foodstuffs, and then roughly working out how much room they'll take. That's simple maths – width x height x depth in metres (so if you have 600 mm wide drawers, 300 mm high and 500 mm deep, it would be $0.6 \times 0.3 \times 0.5 = 0.09$ square metres). You don't have to be that precise, but it does help to know you have planned a place for everything. It makes unpacking much easier and means you aren't left trying to squeeze something into a too-small spot, messing up your new design.

The storage solutions in this kitchen were pretty sweet and discreet. There's a pull-out and powered appliance drawer housing the toaster and coffee maker; above this is the microwave, while underneath are the pots and pans drawers. The drawers under the main preparation bench contain the bin, an integrated dishwasher and an assortment of kitchen-y things, with draining lines being carved into the top of the bench to allow for water to run back into the sink rather than onto the floor. Flat, matt white subway tiles with grey grout add an extra dimension to the kitchen splashback, and run all the way to the ceiling.

Left: A heavy-duty drawer runner ensures appliances can tuck back neatly into the cupboard when not in use.

Below: A small area of benchtop, opposite the fridge and pantry, is useful for dropping groceries before putting them away.

THE BATHROOM

The main bathroom needed a reasonable amount of attention – most of it was cosmetic, but I did have to do a little work on the ceiling to even things out. The ceiling was high, but a structural beam running along the top of one of the walls ruined the symmetry of the room.

The first thing I suggested was to make sense of the appearance of the beam by creating a series of bulkheads the same depth and height as the supporting beam on the other walls. The same was done in the toilet, creating a really neat solution to something that was actually more architecturally obstructive than interesting.

That's the thing with architectural challenges; sometimes cover-ups can actually highlight things that might otherwise be seen as drawbacks. The key is to figure out which bits to be non-apologetic about and which things need to be covered, replicated or disguised.

WORKING WITH WHAT YOU HAVE

Apart from that, the bathroom was more in need of a lift than anything else. It had a lovely original bath and vanity, but they were worn from years of use, as were the marble tiles. The bath and vanity were resprayed with enamel – a great way to freshen up a bathroom quite economically and easily. If we'd had to pull out the bath, that would have meant removing tiles, dealing with waterproofing and a whole raft of expenses and time delays. We didn't change tapware and accessories, as they were in working order and were quite a sweet and appropriate shape and style.

The floor and wall tiles were buffed and regrouted, and sealed, so that the new marble surface will be protected for several more years. Both resurfacing solutions will need to be redone every so often; it's worth weighing up if the short-term fix is better than a complete renovation.

A new border tile and feature tile continue above the existing wall tiles right up to the ceiling. They tie in with what was already there, and look as if they were always meant to be.

Often with renovations, the process is about working out what you can repair or adjust, what needs to go, and what needs to be brought in. This bathroom had a few off notes, including an old wall heater that was not terribly energy efficient and certainly wasn't beautiful. The wall fittings were that sort of Hollywood-style strip lighting down each side of the mirror, which is all well and good when it's fresh and young; the mirror, too, was a little past its prime. A new vanity mirror, plus a new floor-to-ceiling mirror in a corner, help make this a more practical space.

The bathroom window was an interesting puzzle. The bathroom door had a lovely frosted pane of glass; this looked elegant and also provided privacy. The funny thing, though, is that the bathroom window is located in the shower recess. It was also clear glass, facing the neighbours and at torso height. My clients' solution was to have a blind over the window, which didn't look great and also wasn't holding up to the wet particularly well. The obvious thing to do was to use the frosted pane detail from the door. A frosted glass film with the same dimensions and pattern was attached – a simple, quick and easy solution.

A swish new glass shower screen replaced the shower curtain, and with that the room was complete. All in all, the bathroom refresh happened within a few weeks with minimal disruption, the only serious inconvenience occurring when the bath and basin were resprayed and the sealant on the tile was drying for a day.

Left: New pencil edge or listello marble tiles separate the existing marble tiles from the new basketweave marble mosaics.

Opposite: The existing bath and basin were resurfaced, giving new life to the space without the hassle and expense of waterproofing and retiling.

THE LOUNGE ROOM

The lounge room ceiling has two beams that run through it, which is all well and good as the cornices run around them, turning them into a vaulted design feature. The issue, though, is that the fireplace is not an even distance from the beams, making the room look a little off-kilter.

With this kind of issue, you're kind of stuck with what you've got, as moving such beams is nigh impossible as well as hugely expensive. The easiest thing to do is lead the eye elsewhere so you don't notice the inconsistency. We went for this option.

The fireplace isn't quite centred on the wall, and sticks out from the wall by about 400 mm. This gave us the perfect opportunity to flank the fireplace with custom-made shelving and cupboards. Apart from disguising a problem, they are also obviously super useful in terms of creating somewhere for the AV equipment. The bookshelves have been put to great use by all of the owner's tomes, which add an air of sophistication to a formal lounge room. The whole effect is simple but stately, and draws the eye away from the beams to the central element, the rather lovely green marble fireplace (see page 59).

Popping a bioethanol fireplace into the unused fireplace alcove was the perfect solution because, as with many old buildings, the chimneys have long since closed. A disused fireplace just looks lonely, so a solution that brings it back to life is well worth investigating.

THE FURNISHINGS AND ARTWORK

There were plenty of pieces of furniture in the lounge and adjoining sitting room that needed to go. Often when I have the first consult with a client, I'll gently prod them about their belongings to see what, if anything, they are wedded to. I might walk up to a particular piece, place my hand on it and say, 'So, tell me the history behind this', to which I will generally get one of two replies. 'It's important to me because my grandmother left it to me' or something of a similarly delicate nature. Or it will be something like, 'Oh, I just hung onto that from my last place', to which my response, if the piece is less than appealing, will be a fairly swift 'OK, let's get rid of it!' For those indispensable sentimental pieces to work in a new scheme, they often need to be massaged or refreshed.

The couch in the sitting room was one such piece. Quite lovely, but not by any standard contemporary, it was a very comfortable and quite elegantly designed old-style loveseat once owned by a onetime colleague of one of my clients. There was a measure of sentimental value to it, but it was bright red. Bright red, you may have noticed, rarely makes its way into my interiors. I feel red is a loud and angry colour, though that is by no means a hard and fast condemnation of it. Other people see it as lush and sexy, evocative of passion and spirit. I see it as hot and overstimulating, so we simply reupholstered it in a lovely donkey grey velvet and kept the existing stuffing. The piece became one of the central elements from which we created the room.

Pretty much everything else left the building. We brought in ottomans to replace the old high-backed wing chairs. A new coffee table and sidetables with accompanying lamps finish the functional furniture requirements for the room.

I used a felted wool rug from my own range to go underneath a lovely grey, round table in the front sitting room, the one blessed with the most amazing of the views in the apartment. Running around the edge of the room is new cantilevered bench seating, which works really well.

Lighting was a simple hero in the living side of the apartment, a modern industrial take on a chandelier, repeated in the sitting, lounge, entry and dining rooms.

Artwork was something I didn't need to be concerned about in this home. I love sourcing art but, because it's so personal and subjective, it does become very hard to source for clients. Thankfully, the walls of this apartment are filled with pictures both old and new, some painted by famous artist friends. The lounge room art was a particularly brilliant statement.

There were plenty of pieces of furniture in the lounge and adjoining sitting room that needed to go.

Opposite: The artwork and sofa were of huge sentimental value to the clients, so everything in the room was changed to work with them.

THE DINING ROOM

The dining room again took the path of working with the good and delivering something better to replace the bad. Old high-backed chairs were replaced with aviator-like, tan leather bucket chairs that suit the clients perfectly. They're just as appropriate for dinner parties as for work; they look beautiful and lift the contemporary appeal of the room. They also lower the line of the dining table so it is much more subtle in the space. A new console table against the bank of windows adds an element of height, but also gives an opportunity to place stacks of books or a floral arrangement. The dining table, parquetry topped and quite regal in presence, has a lovely amount of wear on it, not damage but patina, which really adds a sense of authenticity. We used a flat weave rug from my own range, which with its geometric pattern, echoes the parquetry and adds extra interest to the space. Again, the mix of old and new, functional and beautiful, really suits the aesthetic of my clients.

THE BEDROOM

The main design challenge in the master bedroom was that, although the view from here is quite spectacular, it could only be seen when you were standing up at the foot of the bed. The clients wanted to be able to open their eyes in the morning and take in that stellar outlook. That meant a little bit of messing around with the layout.

There are only two walls without an external opening, which meant we had two choices for the robe. As you walk into the room, you get a fair amount of view that we didn't want to obstruct, so the wall where the bed used to be located was ruled out. That meant the wall that faced the view, the same wall where you would logically put the bed if you wanted to look outward, was our only option for the wardrobe. Our solution was to sit the bed away from the beautiful new robes, with a bedhead that contains drawers for day-to-day clothing requirements on one side, and a walkway between the robe and drawers. There is thankfully enough room in the space to make this solution work, and having a central bed, like an island in the middle of the room, works perfectly.

Bedside tables were built into the bedhead, the idea being to create more floor area to compensate for the bed taking up more of the room.

Apart from that, it was just a matter of restuffing the upholstered bench seat as it worked with the existing blind, and a chair was added in the corner to be that spot to throw clothes on or sit and tie your shoelaces before heading out into your day.

Throughout the sleeping half of the apartment, the carpet was replaced with a simple cream and white, modern wool carpet that blends nicely with the window treatments we were to work around. This one is a large felted wool loop, which has a sort of uniformly bumpy but very soft appeal underfoot. It feels plush too, unlike the tighter looped carpets that can sometimes feel harsh and commercial. Cut pile carpets have a similarly plush feel underfoot but their major drawback is that when the pile falls with use, pooling happens. Fibres in one section fall one way and in another section, they fall in a different direction. It makes the carpet look as if it has a huge watermark, and I try to avoid them for this reason.

Left: Previously looking at neighbouring properties, the bed now faces towards the amazing harbour view.

Opposite: Mirrored robes with sliding doors serve to double the views.

Painting

A SUBTLE USE OF COLOUR

Not all homes scream for colour. In fact, some clients best suit a subdued or monochromatic palette. In the process of creating the overall look of this home, we went towards a look that was clean, crisp and refined. One piece of reference that came into our view was of an amazing Parisian apartment with parquetry floors and an otherwise entirely white palette. An *entirely* white palette takes a lot of restraint to create and to live in. It's a brilliant showpiece if you're the kind to present your home like a gallery with everything in the right place. My clients, however, aren't like that. They're practical and live in their home without any fanfare. Their apartment serves its purpose during the week and, when the weekend comes, they find themselves elsewhere. The utility of the home comes before the idealism of the perfect white apartment.

That said, the white palette worked super well in this apartment. The relief from all that white, though, comes in the form of the other elements in the space, such as the timber, the charcoal kitchen cabinets and grey upholstery.

I put other colours forward to the clients, more in the darker or mid-toned greens, duck eggs and putties. They felt they were a little too dark and thought the result could be oppressive. When I'm creating homes for other people I always need to respect and consider their point of view about such things as colours, patterns or materials. I can guide as best I can, but I never insist. I can talk about benefits and drawbacks, but ultimately if the client feels strongly for or against something, the home is theirs and they are the ones who enjoy or endure the result. In this instance, the wall colours were toned back to varying degrees of off-whites and the client was happy. Unfortunately, the darker colour would have been the better choice in one room. The clients now agree with that, but the painters have long since left and that adjustment will probably need to wait another ten years.

My advice here is to take a risk. The worst that can happen is you don't like it and have to repaint the room. Or you could love the result. With white palettes, walls of colour in the mid or dark tones give a brilliant contrast and make the whites pop. There's a lot to gain from a light palette, especially if you have low light or are going for a really pure look.

Opposite: The artwork with a sailing theme hangs next to the view of Rushcutters Bay.

Opposite: The potted yucca in the lounge adds a dramatic, sculptural element.

Adding an extra layer

MESHING COLOURS AND TEXTURES

Painting walls isn't the only way to add colour and contrast. Everything you bring into the space is a chance to knit elements together, to highlight some and downplay others.

The floors, previously a kind of standard orangey yellow lacquer, provided an opportunity to bring in another colour. Under the awful lacquer, when sanded back, the timber was a lovely soft sand colour, which played beautifully into the desaturated scheme. When the colour was revealed, the clients and I both decided it was too lovely to change in any way. A staining product called Bona Naturale was used to keep the feel and colour of raw, sanded timber. The wood looks as if it's been freshly cut, but is protected from damage from spills or stains. The timber type will change how a stain reacts, so if you're planning to use one, get your sander to test a small patch before staining the whole floor.

Artworks were a gift to this project. The one in the lounge room is massive. Not *the* biggest artwork I've seen in my projects, but definitely in the top three. It had plenty of colour and also a gold frame; it was a huge statement in the room, so each other element in the room needed to be toned back to a degree to let the painting shine. That meant choosing donkey grey for the sofa and soft pistachio for the ottomans. The rest of the furniture sits in the bronze or gun metal range. The fixed mirror above the fireplace also had a gold painted frame that I changed to match the sofa colour, but in a metallic finish. This leaves the picture frame to be the single golden standout in the room.

The rug adds a textured layer to the room, a traditional looking sisal that felt just right for the formal nature of the space. Echoing the top of the dining table, parquetry is seen in the coffee table, which adds yet another textural and traditionally patterned element.

We wanted the cushions for the built-in cantilevered window seating in the sitting room to somehow echo the kitchen tiles. The palette, again white and grey, was punctuated with a soft, desaturated olive green accented against a white lattice laser cut fabric. That one touch of pattern in the sitting room space was enough to liven up the room and tie in this space at one end of the apartment to the kitchen tiles on the floor at the other end.

LINKING ELEMENTS

It sounds strange, I suppose, to say that I'm linking the furthest ends of a home in a *cushion*, but this is the power of the principles behind adding an extra layer. By understanding the importance of looking at elements for cues and clues as to what else to add, you can dissect the space into some of its core foundations. For this project we have grey, white, timber, metals and Moroccan patterning. Other projects are made up of different elements, but the principle is the same. Find the things that stand out and work together as part of a story that reflects you, your life and your loves, and use those to inform decisions elsewhere in the project. It might be a texture, a colour, a pattern or a material, but using a different amount of the same type of inclusion will help you tie things together in your space, making everything feel as if it belongs.

Focal points

Uniting all the elements will create continuity within your space, but it's important that not everything fits perfectly into a neat little box that you have ticked when doing your design and sourcing. Some things need to stand out. Some things need to engage you. Some things need to attract your eye and draw you into the space to take a closer look.

The art in a home is obviously a great way to draw the eye. The *view*, though, in this apartment is a huge focal point. The sitting room has been brought to life by framing the view, while the new layout of the bedroom lets the owners take the view in as soon as they wake up.

Each room has a focal point, but they're not necessarily the same for everyone. The kitchen benches, for example, might be the thing that attracts one person's attention, the cupboards another, the oven another. For my money, the charcoal and glass cupboards really draw my eye and make the kitchen pop by contrasting with all the white.

Don't misunderstand the need for a focal point. There's nothing wrong with playing down the impact of a space if that's your style. There's a certain tranquillity in having a pared-back life and home, so in these types of spaces you add more subtle points of drama or impact. The dining room, for example, had a lovely floral arrangement as the centrepiece of the old parquetry table. It catches your eye as you breeze through the space; in fact, you only really think about the flowers if they're not there. It's that old adage, you don't know what you've got till it's gone; sometimes you also don't know you need it until you see it. Focal points add that extra bit of punch to a good room.

Below: A very simple neutral palette is brought to life with a cascading central floral arrangement and vibrant orchids in bloom.

The lounge room also is a good example of the plant as a focal point. Without the massive potted yucca, which was formerly outside on the terrace, the room was lovely, but *with* the potted plant, well, it was more dramatic and a little bit more sculptural and wild (see page 83). Maybe that's the best way to think about focal points in a sedate space, perhaps they are like a cat among the pigeons, sent in to create a little ruckus and liven up the place.

DECORATION

Decoration, it seems, is something that people still need to be shown is important. With all the TV shows and magazines around, you'd think you'd notice that the best, most beautiful rooms are put together with finesse, with the right books, the most suitable type of flowers, the candles in the right place, the vignettes made in just the right way to be the perfect little photograph.

It's true, people don't live in photographs. People live in homes and there's no point trying to make your home look like a three-dimensional representation of a magazine shoot. There's no comfort in that; you have to live so obsessively that life just becomes a little bit less fun.

That said, decoration is the part that every homeowner should *want* done right. Decoration should be the last piece of the puzzle, the final flourish that actually most reflects their personality. Sometimes that is precisely the issue. As I said, the clients here are brilliant, easy, wonderful and practical people. No fuss was ever made over any issue or inclusion, everything was smooth sailing – but that

Left: A potted fern, new sidetables and lamps elevate the look of the room.

Above: Vignettes of items, both decorative and practical, add interest to the coffee table.

Opposite: Books, plus a decent smattering of favourite pieces, help enliven the lounge room.

pragmatic approach to life, unsurprisingly, also flows into their approach to living.

The words 'Enough cushions and no more lamps, we have enough lamps' were used. It was like an arrow to my pulsing, designer heart. I think it actually bled, not blood of course, some fabulous glittery substance like the fairy dust used to sprinkle over all these design projects. The fairy dust that makes books arrange themselves in just the right way to play with heights and colours to make bookshelves look 'just so'. The fairy dust that places the candle on the book on the tray next to the vase with the perfectly coloured flowers that tie in with that special painting.

But no. My clients weren't having a bar of it. Don't get me wrong. I chose all the furniture, and even the bed linen was part of the scope … just not that final sparkle.

So I had to bring in a little to liven up the place for the purpose of including it in this book. That's not cheating *exactly*, in fact it's very common to bring in a few things here and there to style a space for a shoot, whether for a book or a magazine, and this project was no different. I just brought in a few more cushions. And lamps.

The things that really light up a space do appear to be frivolous: but candles, plants, cushions and throws do all add something special to a project. Though I swear if I had to stand up and put my hand on my heart and pledge to the design gods that decoration was important, sure I'd feel a little self-conscious, but I could do it honestly.

It's happened before that I've styled a home with that little bit extra for a shoot and then warned the client that they probably shouldn't see what I've done, as it might look better than they were used to. Sure enough, when they'd seen the result when I changed a few cushions and added some flowers, they wanted to keep every last thing. And that's the beauty of taking this gently, gently approach to leading clients into the joys of styling – when they see the home the way I see the home, completed and beautiful, they almost always buy a large portion of those last few things brought in for the day. So it's not cheating at all really, and I bled glitter for nothing.

This home is all about the view, with the cantilevered bench seating offering the perfect vantage point.

CARLOS RUIZ ZAFÓN   THE PRISONER OF HEAVEN

BAUHAUS

BILL CLINTON GIVING

Pieces of the puzzle

BEDTIME STORIES

Anyone who's worked with me on a photoshoot can attest to the fact that one of my most loathed tasks is dressing beds. It's not hard work by any means, but I hate making beds purely because there's an art to it. And it's an art I'm not necessarily inclined towards naturally. It takes some time to get the right look to suit the house. You need to choose colours and textures to suit your theme and, frankly, in my own home, I'm lucky to even make my bed, let alone spend all that time making it perfect.

As a side note for everyone at home, life is far too short to iron sheets, but on these photoshoots we used a steamer to get the linen looking smooth and crease-free once we'd put it on the bed. It's far easier than trying to find a place to hang sheets up and smooth them out.

As far as putting together an elegant bed, there is not a one-style-fits-all solution. Some homes have a relaxed vibe so the beds need to be dressed to suit. Others will be traditional or classic and need a more refined and somewhat uptight solution, almost hotel-like, which is far from rumpled and relaxed. Some will need colour and movement, others will be monochromatic or neutral. To help you – and me too – I've put together a few different looks using the same bed. The next time I'm on a photoshoot, I can simply colour by numbers to achieve a presentable look, no matter what style I'm aiming to create.

You can change the look of a whole room with cushions, pillows, linen and bedcovers. We start with the same room, the same bed, the same occasional furniture and art, but you'll see the change that can be achieved in the look and feel of a room by simply changing the approach a little.

Tucked

This is our starting point, a simple tucked solution. White and grey with a touch of the same duck egg blue from the walls, this look is your basic lick-and-stick solution I think anyone could live with every day. It's fine and practical, but not particularly wonderful.

For this look we have:

- 1 silver/grey fitted sheet
- 1 white flat sheet for contrast
- 1 grey/silver bedcover tucked into the bed with the top sheet
- 1 grey standard pillowcase to match the fitted sheet
- 2 silver pillowcases to match the bedcover
- 1 accent standard pillowcase in velvet to tie in with the wall colour

With the bedcover tucking under the mattress, this look is very structured. The pillows are somewhere between ordered and asymmetrical with some variation, but nothing too exciting or challenging.

Relaxed

If you're the type of person who wants to tumble out of bed and not worry too much about how your bed looks, this look, surprisingly, is not for you. Making a bed look this relaxed takes time. The balance of filling the space correctly, getting the right balance of colours and having that tousled, I-don't-really-care-how-the-bed-looks look is one of the hardest to achieve.

The artful pillow placement is the tricky part. The main thing is to keep to a simple colour and texture palette. This look is entirely made up of knitted wools and linen, so the rest of the interest comes from the placement and layering of tousled texture.

In this look we have a palette of five colours: natural (or wheat), grey, denim blue, white and duck egg blue.

The pieces you'll need to replicate this look are:

- 2 wheat-coloured linen euro pillows
- 1 grey 45 cm square linen pillow
- 1 denim blue linen standard pillow
- 1 white linen lumbar pillow
- 1 wheat linen fitted sheet
- 1 denim blue linen flat sheet
- 1 light grey linen king size (or super king if you can) bedcover
- 1 grey cable knitted woollen throw
- 1 duck egg blue cable knitted woollen throw

The placement is vital here – that sounds very serious I know, but if you want to get this look right, it's all in the details. None of the pillows sit upright – they're all sitting back on an angle and at angles to each other. To get this look predictably each time, having one euro in each rear corner gives you a nice shape and height on the outside, and lets you fill in the gaps with the other pillows in front.

The standard denim blue pillow sits roughly between the two euros, tucking behind the left one and running over the front of the right.

The grey one sits in front of the left euro, while the white lumbar is in front of the standard. The repetition of the square shape on the left with the rectangles one in front of the other in the middle and right makes the haphazard look feel balanced. Each pillow is slightly at an angle to the others, which also helps create a relaxed look.

The bedcover and sheets are softly crumpled so you get some wavy movement. We steamed out hard creases from the linen to stop it looking messy.

The throws are strewn over each other at angles to the rest of the bedcovers. This is a great way to break up the expanse of the bedcover, and having a king or super king cover means you have a generous amount of fabric flowing off the side of the bed and pooling on the floor.

Asymmetrical

This look is more structured but not traditional. You can see a few different approaches to this one in this book – the asymmetrical look is probably one with more possibilities than most.

Creating an asymmetrical look is about playing with shapes and stacking them in different ways. In this instance we have:

- 1 champagne-coloured standard pillow
- 1 champagne-coloured velvet euro pillow
- 1 blush velvet standard pillow
- 1 blush euro pillow
- 1 faux fur 45 cm square accent cushion
- 1 champagne-coloured cotton fitted sheet
- 1 blush flat cotton sheet
- 1 blush velvet bedcover
- 1 silver velvet bedcover
- 1 blush woollen throw

There's no one answer to getting an asymmetrical look to work, but some simple ways to play with it for yourself are to experiment with the way the cushions are stacked – some might face forward, while you can try stacking others on top of the other. Think about the shape of the pillows – rectangles look good in front of each other; squares look good in front of other squares.

Try not to use too many pillows and cushions. I've used five here, and you can get up to six or seven if you're using some smaller ones, but you don't want the pillows to creep too far forward and cover the bed.

In this instance, we have two euros on the right side stacked in front of one another, with two standard pillows sitting on top of each other on the left hand side. We have one accent cushion, 45 cm square, that looks appropriate in front of the euro as the shapes relate well to each other.

The bedcovers and sheets are neat and smoothly made with nice straight lines. Part of the interest comes from the variation of shapes in the pillows and cushion, but it's also from the different textures and colours of the bedcovers, which have been folded over each other to give a strip of one colour in the fitted sheet, another in the top sheet – in this instance the same colour (blush) but different texture (velvet) on the first bedcover and the same texture but different colour (silver) on the second one.

The sheets are all neatly folded back and in line with each other. There are no crumples or ruffles – nice smooth, flat and ordered is the approach here. However, there's no harm in combining a relaxed look and asymmetrical pillow arrangement.

Textured

The idea here is all about variation of size, shape, colour and texture. There's a simple colour palette, in this instance, greys, browns, copper and navy. There are patterns, textures, metallics, more patterns and different materials such as velvet, cotton and natural fibres.

Again, we have two types of bedcovers used, one folded over the other. Both have a pattern – one has a velvet texture and the other a smooth sateen cotton. The two colours complement each other and the patterns aren't too wildly dissimilar.

The aim is for an unstructured, relaxed look, but using a more varied colour and materials palette.

I've used one of each kind of cushion:

- 1 silver/fitted sheet
- 1 white flat sheet for contrast
- 1 navy and wheat euro pillow
- 1 copper-patterned 45 cm square accent cushion
- 1 brown patterned lumbar pillow
- 1 standard grey and white patterned pillow to match the bedcover
- 1 grey velvet medallion euro to match the second bedcover
- 1 grey velvet medallion standard pillow to match the second bedcover
- 1 navy textured 45 cm square cushion

This look was the one I was least enthusiastic about creating as I thought it might look haphazard and thrown together, but it actually works very well.

There's a sense of order in the placement of the pillows and cushions. On the left, rectangles are in front of rectangles and, on the right, squares are in front of squares. Smaller cushions are in front, resting at an angle to lower their line even further, allowing your eye to be drawn towards the bedcovers. There's plenty of visual interest, with the cushions complementing or contrasting with each other; texture is layered on texture, with the bedcovers adding more texture and pattern. The bedcovers don't add extra colour, allowing the cushions to remain the hero. It's a bit like the make-up rule of either accenting the eyes or the lips. If you accent neither you get no impact; if you accent both, you have a visual fight on your hands.

Traditional

One of the simplest looks to achieve, the traditional symmetrical arrangement is tried and true, and there are only a few variations on it. The idea of this look is order and structure. You'll need two of everything so in this look we have:

- 1 white fitted sheet
- 1 black-bordered white flat sheet
- 2 plain white cotton standard pillows
- 2 white-with-black-border euro pillows
- 2 black 45 cm square accent cushions
- 2 gold-studded velvet lumbar pillows

There are a few possibilities to achieve a traditional style. For example, you could have two euros at the back, two standards on each side, stacked one on top of the other, and one feature cushion in front. In the look shown here, I wanted to have both the black for contrast against the white, and the gold for interest, to elevate it from a palette of safe and simplified black and white.

Here we've used only high thread count, high quality cotton or cotton sateen sheets of the type you might find in a hotel. A symmetrical layout works well with a hotel look, but you can opt for linens with this arrangement to soften the look to great effect.

We have two standard cushions at the rear, sitting upright behind the euros. The euros sit in front with the square black accent cushions centred in front and the gold lumbar pillows in the front row.

The bedcovers are folded back, with the top sheet sitting just in front of the cushions. There's plenty going on, so no feature throws are used, but in this instance I used bed linen that had an interesting black band that complemented the bedcover and euros perfectly.

It's interesting to note how the bed frame and the room around it doesn't change in any of these iterations, but the look and feel of the room does.

The bed itself looks different; in some instances the metal frame takes on a hipster look, in others a refined old world elegance or a more hard-edged industrial feel. If you're wanting to freshen up your room and don't want to change the structure, furniture or colour, you can play around with creating some of these looks for yourself.

The best thing is that if you buy the linen and cushions you need for some, or all, these different approaches, you can change the feeling of your space from month to month or even week to week with little more effort than it takes to change the sheets on your bed on washing day.

Warehouse conversion

HOME FOR A FAMILY AND AN ART COLLECTION

The brief

Warehouses are made to work. Big and expansive, they are never full of creature comforts, luxury inclusions or beautiful things. They are set up as places to create or construct. It's fitting, then, that a prominent artist creating Archibald Prize–winning pieces over a long and productive career used to work here.

When the warehouse was passed on to his son (who was married with one child and another on the way), the intention was to create a home for a growing family. They wanted to relieve it of its hard-working duties and give it a little bit of TLC and a facelift. One of the main things was that most of the spaces in it were far too big to be liveable, so they had to be reconfigured by the architect. I was called in to give those spaces the character they deserved, and help turn the warehouse into a family home.

Right: The hard-working skeleton of the warehouse shows through its beautiful new skin.

Opposite: Stairs lead down to the garage from a sitting area adjoining the open-plan dining and living spaces.

Structure

BACKGROUND

This building is a rare find. Truly huge in proportion, it occupies the entire block, which is almost impossible to find with our present land to property ratios. It's very hard, too, to find warehouses that haven't been turned into townhouses or smaller apartments. This place is a real gem.

Fairly rustic skylights, blacked out to protect artworks from sun damage, were fitted into the exposed truss ceilings. Brickwork does its job in holding the place up, but also creates a perfect backdrop for the raw and utilitarian renovation of a cavernous space.

Everywhere you looked there was opportunity, and the architect for the job, Julian Brenchley of the television program *The Block* fame, reconfigured a space he had originally designed decades earlier. It must be quite interesting to have designed a home for the father and then get to reimagine it for the son. It does go a long way to show you exactly the point we're getting at with this book – that every home changes to suit its owners.

Homes, although substantial and relatively immoveable objects, are not static. They shake off their old skin and settle in to suit the needs of a new occupant. This transformation can happen dramatically and quickly; at other times, the home can slowly evolve, with tweaks and changes happening in a way that suits the finances and desires of the homeowner.

This evolution was special in a number of ways. The first time around, the architect designed a space with lots of art storage, a dark bedroom downstairs next to the art studio, and a bathroom and laundry tacked together in the

adjoining room. From there, a staircase led to an open-plan kitchen, living and dining room area in a space big enough to house another sitting area next to an outdoor terrace.

The terrace was not the most inviting space, but it did give the opportunity to get outside and see the sky and treetops. It was, in fact, the only connection to the outside as the building was hemmed in on all sides by brick walls with no external windows.

The warehouse was not much to look at from the street. It felt like the kind of place that, unless you knew the secret password, you wouldn't get past the heavy roller door. Down a long alleyway lined with neighbours' garage doors, all you can see of the home is a front door, a metal garage door and a bit of brickwork. In terms of entrance appeal, unless you like the look of garbage bins and roller doors, it really left a lot to be desired.

Inside, the warehouse was similarly utilitarian, with concrete, brick and not much else. Even so, there was something about it and, funnily enough, I have known about this place for a long time and in its various incarnations. Many years ago I attended a party thrown by the son for his dad. It was a happy occasion and I saw the warehouse as a home and place of joy and life. When I visited a few years later, the downstairs studio space had been converted into a film set for *The Block* judging reveals as well as the behind-the-scenes, when I was on the couch with fellow judges Shaynna and Neale, talking about the weekly goings-on.

FINDING THE LIGHT

Everywhere you looked, the place had potential – a tactful way to say that there was room for improvement. With no external openings and the skylights closed in, however, the first port of call was to open up the outside to let light in.

The architect did this in a number of ways. Firstly, he installed operable skylights, and also created a lightwell at one end of the building, which gave all four bedrooms windows. This allows air to circulate as well as letting light into previously dark and uninhabitable places.

On the opposite side of the building to the new lightwell was the uninviting terrace, which was partially hidden behind a low wall of glass doors and fixed panels. This let in some light, but the architect turned what was an add-on into the major feature of the room. He did this by opening up the entire wall, all the way up to the raked ceilings, with a wall of black metal and glass that reflected the trusses overhead.

The lady of the family thought a Juliet balcony off the terrace and overlooking what was to be either a big family room or a showroom for their lovely old Porsche would be the final touch to bring the terrace to life. She was right. The outdoor space now beckons people to connect with the sky and the view of the trees in neighbouring yards, and gives the new lounge room a lovely green outlook.

THE LAYOUT

The layout changed simply but sensibly. The upstairs living area was increased by rotating and relocating the staircase and, instead of it being U-shaped, has it run in one long line between the garage and lounge room, landing next to the kitchen and dining area. Steel handrails, painted black, work perfectly with the industrial feel of the warehouse, and tie in with the trusses and terrace windows.

Where the staircase used to be, a space was created as an overflow entertainment place for pre-dinner drinks, or a place to sit and read in one of those rare moments when the kids are napping. The adjacent dining area sits between the sitting area and the study, which spans the full width of the lightwell windows.

The lightwell also has the same black folded steel profile. Carving this shaft, and letting fresh air and light into the building, allowed the layout to sustain a bedroom at each rear corner of the warehouse, two up and two down or, if you prefer, two on the left and two on the right, creating a nice symmetry to the home.

The layout also evolved to create an ensuite bathroom for each bedroom, finally making sense of the enormous space downstairs that had previously been home to stacks and stacks of extremely valuable artwork.

Cars are a passion of the man of the house, and therefore the garage is important to him. The family has an old Porsche as well as their two everyday cars, and this helped decide the layout downstairs.

The garage is large enough to fit four cars, but the cool thing is the space next to it. This was formerly the art studio and then our film studio, which the owners wanted to leave relatively open to showcase the old '70s Porsche that deserved pride of place (see page 113). The challenge was to get the car elegantly in and out of the space through a set of slightly oversized folded steel and glass doors – the solution was to install a turntable that allows the car to simply drive in, spin around and head straight into the massive space that the lounge and sitting spaces overlook. Every day, when the owners arrive home and walk up their staircase they can take in the beautiful lines of the Porsche from multiple angles as they climb.

Everywhere you looked the place had potential – a tactful way to say that there was room for improvement.

Opposite: The home office space, behind the dining area, is perched on the side of the lightwell, which allows for good working conditions.

Below: A butler's pantry is tucked away neatly behind dark doors.

Opposite: Along with the marble splashback, the fluted glass doors and industrial lighting all add interest to the kitchen.

Design elements

A TRUE COLLABORATION

It's fair to say the success of this project comes in equal parts from the architect's vision, the clients' requirements, the warehouse structure and the need to display a serious art collection. Far from fighting with each other, the agenda of each element allowed for a cohesive and resolved approach, resulting in a really amazing home.

Being the exec producer of *The Block*, and my part-time boss, the client has a lot of experience in development. With his knowledge and experience come very well informed opinions. Because of my love of joinery, I was engaged at the beginning of the project. Bespoke cabinetry was one of the big focuses and the owner wanted my input into the space for this purpose as well as making sure there weren't any missed opportunities in the bathroom layouts.

After working up a few details for the kitchen and bathrooms and collating some ideas for fittings and fixtures, the project was handed back to the architect to flesh out with the clients directly. The result you see today is about 99 per cent the architect/client collaboration in terms of the wet areas and kitchen, with my initial plans being the framework they built from, but adjusting things as they went due to time or budget constraints.

The idea was to create an interior that worked with the exterior, that sat like a fresh new skin inside this old, functional structure but was not so modern and cold that it felt as if it didn't belong. To achieve that, the materials used included exposed brick, encaustic patterned tiles, copper, brass, herringbone sisal and touches of high luxury in the form of marble in the kitchen and bathrooms.

Opposite: The upstairs living areas overlook the gallery space, which features a car as well as artwork.

The family has an old Porsche as well as their two everyday cars, and this helped decide the layout downstairs.

There wasn't much exchange of images or reference. The architect and owner have known each other since childhood and have worked together for years, and so have developed a swift shorthand understanding of each other's ideas. My involvement came back into play after the structure was built and it came time to make this shell a home.

THE IMPORTANCE OF COMMUNICATION

Getting to know my clients is an important part of my job, and it's just as important for the clients to get to know me. I don't have to take on all projects that come my way, so when I'm meeting a client for the first time, I am assessing them as much as they are assessing me. In this case, I didn't have to do that, as I've known the client for years — not that that is necessarily a guarantee of everything going to plan.

Being clear on a common goal and working towards the realisation of, at times, a lifelong dream is a precious thing to be responsible for, and taking on the right clients is as important as them taking on the right designer. If I, for a second, believe what the client wants doesn't suit my skillsets, I'll recommend someone I think might be better suited to the task. Thankfully, the clients I do get to work with are always a great fit and working towards a common goal is a relatively intuitive process.

If you're planning to work with a designer, you should aim to have that kind of relationship — creating a home together is one of the most challenging and wonderful experiences you're ever likely to have, and should never be otherwise.

A MATTER OF SCALE

Feeling my way through choices is part of the puzzle. The other part, though, is more scientific. The spaces will dictate what sorts of things are needed for the home to function the way the homeowners want it to. In this case, the spaces are truly cavernous, and so the dining table had to be three metres long and the sofas 2.8 metres. This sort of scale doesn't leave that many options, and when you filter those through the aesthetic considerations of the brief, the choices are whittled down even more. That helps to lock in the building blocks of each space so you're working around the thing with the tightest constraint.

After you work out what those big pieces are, it's simply a matter of trying different configurations of occasional furniture to create interest where you need it. You might try different sidetables with different lamps, and then the coffee table may be the same line as the other pieces in the room, or perhaps contrast strongly by introducing another period or style as a central piece. The rug and cushions may coordinate with other choices, and décor items are then used to tie a room together.

Opposite: Prized artworks fit neatly by the desk. Note the custom copper finger pull on the desk drawer.

Below: The office space adjoins the master bedroom, and shares the lightwell with it.

The spaces will dictate what sorts of things are needed for the home to function the way the homeowners want it to.

INSTALLATION

We had to install everything here in two days. That's one day for delivery and the other for set-up ready to be lived in. In anyone's world that's not much time, but funnily enough these projects, where everything is ordered and organised and coordinated so that all the furniture, art, décor, linen and flowers come together quickly, are quite refreshing. It means I can think about what I want the whole home to look like all the way down to the smallest detail and then get a few extra sets of hands, some good removalists to help move things around and a team of great suppliers and the job is done with minimal mess and fuss. Well, actually lots of mess with packaging materials having to be removed and disposed of, but that's beside the point.

Sourcing this project was a very structured and thoroughly organised undertaking. It was done exactly the way I always tell people to – every single piece was found, they were all put on hold while the details were fleshed out, I made sure everything was available for the install date, and all the items were immediately locked away once they were finally decided on.

Original industrial lights with glass covers, appropriate to such a space, hang over the dining table.

Below: A touch of green and a view of the sky make the home office an inviting space.

Opposite: Simple coffee table styling 101 – two stacks of books, a sculptural object and something living.

Some thoughts on sourcing

A lot of my sourcing is done online, first finding the products on my suppliers' websites. I've started sourcing in a really broad manner, slowly whittling the look down to the final products by seeing which pieces work best together. This means making, on our server, a folder titled 'Images' for each project. Into this folder go a lot of smaller folders. I save a pdf print of the page of the item that catches my eye as well as a picture of the item, both titled with the name of the product, in a folder named with the supplier's company name. I do this over and over until I have an ordered and very, very full reference of any possible thing that might work for the project. I end up with up to five times the number of options I actually need. I then put pages together with my favourite pieces, starting with something like a sofa and then lay out the room on the page, placing a sidetable, lamp, coffee table or whatever that type of room requires to see what works best. I keep doing this until I have pages of options, sometimes changing the sofa or reconfiguring the whole look with completely new items to see which one will work best.

After the design has been agreed upon, I contact suppliers and ask them which pieces are available. Once that's confirmed, the pieces are quoted, and pricing is provided to the clients for approval. Sometimes this means replacements have to be found at the eleventh hour because of cost. Generally, though, as I know the client's budget, I will have sourced items from places that will more or less match that budget – just doing that saves me a lot of time, and is the smartest way to do it.

118

Making use of an awkward space, a sitting area fits neatly between the main lounge and dining areas, with views out to neighbouring rooftops.

Opposite: Encaustic floor tiles, along with hexagonal marble wall tiles and marble shower niches, contrast beautifully with the industrial plumbing fittings and black metal towel rails.

Rooms under the spotlight

For this project, one of my main tasks was to focus on the furniture. I concentrated on the lounge room upstairs, the big open space downstairs, a sitting area, the dining area, a study and the master bedroom. The outdoor space also needed some work, and all these parts of the house obviously needed to tie in with each other. That meant locking in as many rooms and as many big items as possible. The size of the spaces here was the main consideration – they are truly cavernous, and dictated the scale of the furniture.

As well as size, the choice of dining table was dictated, of course, by personal taste. The chunky pale timber table looks just right in the space. There were plenty of options for the dining chairs, but we settled on tan leather carvers for one side and a timber bench matching the table on the other. This creates a nice asymmetry to the table, which works well with the raked ceiling and asymmetrical line of the room. The different height levels also mean there is a sense of perspective, with the bench being lower than the backs of the carvers, which lead your eye up to the artwork behind and the lighting above.

The sitting space is composed of comfortable and colourful furniture, mostly chosen to create a point of difference in the unusual space. Sofas wouldn't have worked as their backs would have either blocked the railing or the view into the space from the lounge or dining areas. The central circular rug gives these four chairs the base they need, while the gold velvet ottoman is that little bit of funk the house just cries out for.

In the master bedroom, relaxed linen is used against metal and industrial formed furniture, and feels right with the exposed brick wall. For such an industrial home, this space really feels inviting and friendly and a little bit luxe.

The bathrooms, too, are that blend of luxury and utility, with exposed brickwork making another appearance, this time set against a palette of encaustic tiles, copper basin and marble tiles. The final flourish comes from the exposed plumbing that snakes down the wall and finishes in matt black tapware. The bathrooms are really heaven on a stick; each one gets a variation on the theme with one having the encaustic tiles, another concrete hex tiles, while another has a simple concrete floor.

The study desk, with all of its black joinery and folded steelwork, calls out for a comfortable and industrial chair. The perfect one brings to mind images of aviation, while its tan leather ties in nicely with the dining chairs nearby.

Outside, a large round timber table is perfect for seating a bunch of friends on the weekend, with grey Malawi chairs adding a beautiful textured element to the space. The wall behind the table is a gallery for pots and plants, which soften the brickwork.

Furniture was chosen to be minimal in impact; colours, textures and materials are all fairly understated, which allows the art, the real star of the home, to shine.

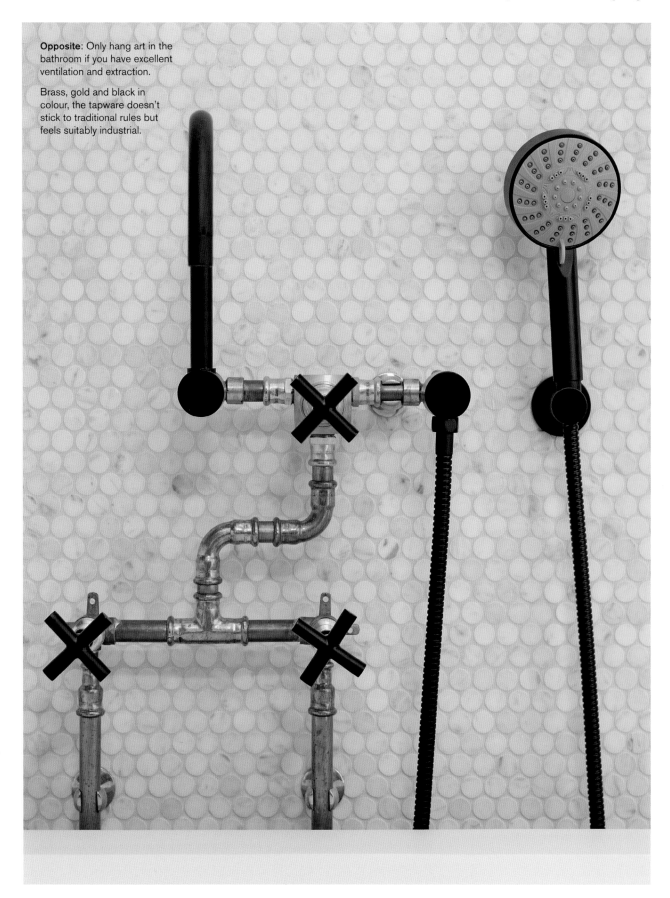

Opposite: Only hang art in the bathroom if you have excellent ventilation and extraction.

Brass, gold and black in colour, the tapware doesn't stick to traditional rules but feels suitably industrial.

Impact

A BACKDROP FOR BOLD COLOUR

With a palette of brown brick, black steel and white paint, the building itself doesn't present much of a colourful statement. The flip side is that it's the perfect palette to add in big punches of colour through rugs, furniture and art.

The rugs in the living spaces are stunners. The one in the lounge is a soft gold that doesn't fight against the pared-back living space. The sitting room rug is perfectly matched to the ottoman and the lilac and gold mohair cushions. This simple addition of colour elevates a grey and white set of choices into something more interesting.

The master bedroom features blues and golds, again the perfect contrast to the brown brick and white walls. The copper electrical conduit snakes down the wall, and is a brilliant architectural pop of extravagance.

The art, though, is the big star. This is the only time that I have used only one artist in a home and, for me, it is probably the most memorable use of art. It's not only the interest and colour these works bring to the home, but also the fact that there is so much history attached to them, reminding the owners of their loved one.

My favourite piece is massive, the biggest artwork I've ever had the pleasure of building a room around. On the wall at one end of the lounge room, it fitted by only a few centimetres. It's dramatic and beautiful; yellows, pinks, apricot and even a touch of red and lilac, as if the home's decorative palette was made just to work in with it. That's one of those happy, informed coincidences that remind me that sometimes the universe is working behind the scenes to make great outcomes happen seamlessly.

Below: Copper piping, mounted onto the rustic brick walls, houses electrical cabling.

Adding an extra layer

BALANCING INDUSTRIAL FEATURES

I generally favour texture over pattern, but there are certain patterns that show up time and again in my work. Herringbone's one I often use, and in this project I didn't even have to include it myself. The floor, chosen by the architect and clients, is a macro, grey oak laid in a herringbone pattern, and is a great base for adding an extra textured and patterned layer to this amazing home.

The extra layer doesn't have to be added at the end; indeed, the most interesting interiors are a series of layers. Details make the difference between the project-home approach and the luxury of the images you see in glossy magazine pages.

Details such as floorboards, patterns and textures, or colours, are a lovely starting point for an interesting and engaging interior. Wall treatments are the same; walls are not just structural or a background for art, but another opportunity to create some texture and a play of light. The brickwork in the warehouse does just that, as do the steel trusses crisscrossing above you in the ceilings upstairs.

You need to be careful in industrial spaces not to go too far with the heavy metal. Too much of a good thing can be overwhelming, so it's a smart idea to also build in some relief. The brickwork and steel form the industrial visual foundation to the home; the perfect foil is in the timber floors and the use of such fabrics as linen and velvet.

Luxury elements also work as a contrast to the industrial – things like the metallic detail of the plumbing or the amazing tapware, or the marble used in the bathrooms and the kitchen. They are hard and raw in the way only elements like stone and metal can be, but are also luxurious in the measured way they are used. Again, with things such as metallic details or even marble, you can go too far; the success of these spaces is in the balance between utilitarian and indulgent. You can have a lot of one *and* a lot of the other – the beauty is in how they can exist in different areas in different ways.

The ceilings, for example, are pure industrial; the lounge room setting pure luxe. The structure of the building is all concrete, timber, steel and glass; to contrast that, the furniture then has to be more natural, more muted in colour and visually easy on the eye with softer edges and no harsh forms.

Opposite: Australian natives light up the space, their more architectural form working well with the structured space.

Focal points

THE IMPORTANCE OF ART

Art really does bring a space to life, the more the better if used in the right way. That's an interesting fact that I've only really understood in the last few years, thanks to some added education from my husband and his love of art. I previously only considered art as decoration, something chosen to suit a room because the colours worked, or because it could be used as a springboard to inform the rest of an interior palette.

Let's face it, not everyone has the time or money to cultivate an art collection and, rather than have bare walls, it's better to buy a beautiful décor piece and match your cushions and rug to it. In fact, that's the way most homeowners go about decorating their own homes and there's nothing wrong with that approach at all.

The challenge with this approach, though, is how to keep your space from looking same-samey – you know, the dreaded result that looks nice and presents well, but has no real sense of self, no real soul. It's the things that are lived in and represent the people in the home, their quirks and eccentricities that really add interest. I think it's a bit like when you get to *really* know someone, such as your best friend or your partner. That person generally presents as a lovely, polite and sociable person, which they are in spades, but when you really get to *know* them, you learn the things that make them tick, that light them up, annoy them or inspire them. It's those insights that draw you closer to them, make you fall in love with them, and it's those very things, too, that do the same thing in a home. When someone is showing their polite acquaintance face, you

may well think they're perfectly lovely. But when they let you in to see the real person inside, you see the beauty and interest and wonderfulness bubbling just below the surface. It's *exactly* the same with a room that reflects more than just a coherent colour scheme with matching art and cushions.

FINDING PIECES WITH MEANING

Art, I've learnt, is best in a room when it means something. When it's found in the streets of Paris while on holiday, while browsing through a gallery looking for a bargain, while you look online for other things and stumble upon an artist or fall in front of the right piece at the right time.

There's an artist I have used a number of times in other people's homes. I still haven't managed to buy one of his paintings, but the last time I was very, very close. I stood before it and my heart started to race. I had a physiological response to an object that literally made my body run faster. *That* is what art is supposed to do to you.

So what if the art doesn't work with your décor? Let me rephrase that. *So what* if art doesn't work with your décor!

So.

Darn.

What.

Art can hang independent of the décor in the rooms or the cushions you love. Art doesn't need to play nicely with the rug. It can be its own hero, a focal piece in any room that works for you and makes *you* feel something.

Left: The orange flames in the painting and the copper basin are particularly dramatic elements.

Below: The entire home features the work of only one artist, the owner's father, with each piece adding something special to the room it occupies.

Why on earth would you want to put a massive artwork in a bathroom? It's not practical and the steam from the shower might destroy it. It's not advisable, but the piece on the brick wall in this home just works so perfectly, who's to say it's wrong? The copper in the hand basin looks as if it was painted with the same colour as the flames in the painting. The colour of the bricks surely borrowed from the oranges in the painting in front of it. It just works. It wasn't chosen because of these fittings, nor were the fittings chosen to work with the artwork.

The massive pastel piece in the lounge room livens up the room; in fact, it livens up that whole side of the house. The piece behind the dining table adds colour and drama and geometry just by being. The small pieces on the desk provide pops of colour and a little pocket of edginess to the workspace that surely would keep you burning the midnight oil just that little bit longer.

Art is the ultimate focal point and although not everyone appreciates the same pieces in the same way, nor does one type fit all or provide a single, go-to answer on the right or wrong way to use it. Art is undeniably the single most telling thing about a homeowner that you can find in their home. So what does your art say about you?

DECORATION

With especially sparse, cavernous and hard-working structures such as this one, that soft layer is particularly important. Yes, furnishings are the big opportunity to soften down the aesthetic of the place, but you need more than that. As you look at the space, walk through it or live in it, you notice every detail, even if not all at once. At various times, you'll take in the whole project, all the bits and pieces in it, the textures, layers and focal points as well as the finer pieces of its overall look and feel.

Subconsciously, you will read the space as a whole, with all its colours, shapes, textures and patterns, and it will have a certain effect on you. The place will feel less homely if you have nothing personal to relate to, no pieces from your travels, no living elements, no touchy-feely sentimentally bits that make you reminisce and daydream of holidays past or dreams of days to come.

In this case, it's also the cascading greenery in the outdoor area that softens the pots and bricks and brings the space to life, beckoning the family outdoors to interact with the trees and sky above. It's the mohair cushions in gold and lilac that tell them it's time to relax and kick their feet up, read a book and stare out at the tops of houses and beyond. It's all the pots and plants and candles and tchotchkes that give you an idea of who lives in a home, what they love, what they want and what they want their life to look and feel like. Make sure when you invite people into your home that you're showing them your true self. Doing anything else is denying them the opportunity to really know you, and that's just denying them the best things in life.

Opposite: A perforated metal sideboard is appropriate in the industrial setting.

Right: Pots, timber and greenery all soften the stone and brick palette.

The oversized sofas, which are 2.8 metres long, and enormous lamps, give a sense of the sheer scale of the home.

Pieces of the puzzle

FLOOR SHOW

You should know by now that I'm not a one-size-fits-all kind of designer. I don't have a set style and don't like to repeat myself from one client to the next. Each room I design suits the home and the client's needs as well as their personality – there's no chance of coming up with the same result twice.

I thought it would be interesting to show you what happens when you change one element in a room. That element is one of the most transformative things you can find in a home, but it's one thing nonetheless.

Rugs make or break a room. In most cases, several different rugs would work in a particular space, but each one would make the room look entirely different. Choosing the right rug, therefore, is an important part of creating your perfect home.

A matter of contrast

We start with my home, my room and my rug. I like the way it sits right under the sofa, demarcating the area for the lounge as well as having a walkway on each side. I like the contrast between the dark rug and the white and grey elements around it. This is a great starting point, demonstrating a flat colour option with a little texture and it's a good-sized rug for this room and this furniture.

The room is 4.3 by 3.5 metres and the sofa about 3.3 metres long. The rug is 3.2 by 2.3 metres, and is made of felted undyed grey wool in a herringbone pattern.

It takes up just under half the floor space, and is only slightly longer than the base of the sofa. If it were any larger, it would interfere with the fireplace and walkways. When choosing a rug to suit a sofa, you want to find one that is big enough to fit entirely under the sofa, with between about 50 and 100 mm clear on each side. If you have the space, look for a rug that gives you around 600 to 700 mm on either side of the sofa – that way it will be wide enough to sit the sidetables on too.

Test pattern

I loved my rug in the room, but love this one even more. While it's smaller, it looks just right, as it sits under the front of the sofa but allows for a little timber floor around the perimeter as well giving a sense of continuity to the room.

The pattern really elevates the interest level in the room and ties in nicely with the artwork, even though they share no common elements. Simply by being bold and interesting, they complement each other, and the simple white and grey palette takes a backseat to the lovely blues, the handmade geometric pattern and the softening effect of the tasselled edges.

In my opinion, this is the right-sized rug and the right amount of interest. It's a great solution for a family rug, its patterning and dark colour helping to hide some of life's accidents.

The laid-back look

Again, this rug is the right size but, being lighter, ties in with the sofa. It also accentuates the coffee table, with the soft grey and white pattern acting as a contrast to the dark metal frame and timber top.

You can see that the two standout features of the room are now the coffee table and the artwork. The rest of the space merges in one neutral and bright friendly space.

This isn't a bad choice for the room if you want a more laid-back and airy look but, with its lack of contrast, it is perhaps a little too bland to really work in this pared-back room. Light rugs, also, aren't great family rugs; although the variation in pattern and colour in this one would hide a little wear and tear, I wouldn't advise it if you have young children or pets.

Pieces of the puzzle

Size does matter

This rug is a good contrast to the coffee table, but feels one size too small. While it fits under the front of the sofa, the amount of timber showing around the perimeter makes it feel less generous than the last option.

The variation in pattern and contrast between the two colours allows it to hide more wear and tear than the previous rug, and it does give the room the same light and airy look, but its size doesn't do the room justice.

Apart from its size, the pattern is great and the colours are really well suited both to this space and the palette of the whole home. The organic nature of the pattern makes the room look very friendly and crisp, but ultimately, it's one of the least successful choices and certainly one of the least practical for this family home.

The wrong scale

Now here's one I can say really doesn't work. The colour and pattern are beautiful and suit the room perfectly, but unfortunately the scale of this rug, again, lets it down.

I know many people reading this will consider the rug to be large compared to the majority of those on offer in rug stores around the country. The simple fact of this space, however, is that it's ruled by a huge sofa, much larger than those in most family homes, so the rug needs to be that much bigger to suit.

Ideally, the rug would occupy more space to the right of the sofa, reducing the amount of floor you see and giving a little breathing space to the arm of the sofa. Unfortunately, this little beauty simply looks a little mean in terms of scale. The opulence of the colour, pattern and texture are not enough to make up for its size, or lack thereof.

Pieces of the puzzle

Hard yards

Here's a perfect example of what happens when you get almost all the elements right in a room, but the result just doesn't add up.

The colour of the nice, natural sisal rug ties in well with the floors and the oak table behind, and its simple and functional flat weave potentially works in the space.

The size, too, is spot on, being bigger than the sofa and allowing enough space to create a walkway as well as giving plenty of space for the coffee table.

The stripe, however, just doesn't work.

The hard contrast is too harsh against the predominantly white and grey palette, and the coffee table legs clash with the stripes beneath. On top of that, the timber floorboards run in a perpendicular direction to the stripes on the rug, which is confusing to the eye.

All this goes to show that colour, pattern, texture, material, size and shape all need to be right for any element in a room to work. And the right elements are only the right elements when they work in harmony with everything else in the space.

New Home

A LESSON IN FAMILY HARMONY

The brief

It really doesn't get more blue sky than this project. My clients – both busy people – were in the final stages of building their forever home for their three young children to grow up in and enjoy. They wanted only one thing, for me to help them create their perfect family home. My approach needed to be comfortable, stylish and appropriate to the architecture, with an emphasis towards practicality in the family spaces and refinement in the adult ones.

Their architect, Tzannes Associates, is one of Australia's best, so it's no surprise that they considered all the common issues people face in their homes and came up with elegant solutions. In some of my jobs, I'm with the clients from the get go, helping them realise their home dreams. This project was different – all the major design and construction decisions had been made, and my task was to work on the interior palette, and to provide ways for the homeowners to relax with their children and spend time with their guests.

The brief was very clear: to create spaces that fitted the different uses for each member of the family and to make the interior finish and design respect the exterior form so carefully crafted by the architect, landscaper and builder.

There were almost two briefs – one involving the adult areas, where the look could be precise and more high maintenance, and the second for the family areas which had to be more practical. A common palette would tie them together. I usually only get to work on family *or* high end at one time, so to do both in one house was amazing. Projects like this are rare, and that makes them very exciting indeed.

Below: Hard-wearing and
practical furniture is used in
the family room.

Opposite: A brick walkway, referencing the bricks used for the house, leads from the front gate into the home.

Structure

ARCHITECTURAL INTEREST

A checklist of great architectural interest might go something like this:

High ceilings
Large openings
Grand proportions
Appealing building design
Ceiling details
Voluminous spaces
Feature staircase
Fireplaces
Orientation to the best outlooks
Entrance appeal

This house ticks every single box.

From the street, you have no idea what you're about to encounter – it's very discreet, and all you can see is a metallic fence, a streamlined garage and understated landscaping. Once inside the gate, though, you know you're somewhere special. A brick pathway leads through the garden to the house, which itself is built of long, narrow bricks, almost Japanese or American mid-century in feel.

The house has been designed to wrap around a particularly beautiful winter magnolia tree (see page 159) that the family love to look at and the children enjoy climbing. The house is huge, but doesn't feel it – it still has a human scale. It works really well now, but as the kids get older, there will be space for them to hide from their parents. It's a real feat to create a home as large and

impressive as this and yet allow it to sit in its environment naturally, as if it was meant to be there all along. One of the first things you notice are the truly massive sliding doors and enormous windows rising up to raked ceilings. These over-scaled openings both soften the building and open it up, so that the inside really does feel connected to the outside and vice versa. In the adult space, the doors and windows are metal, while in the family area, they're blackbutt framed with brass detailing – it's interesting to use such different components in the one house, but it is a clever way of demarcating the spaces.

CEILINGS AND STAIRCASES

Ceilings are high throughout, which is glorious – you'll know what I'm talking about if you've ever moved from a place with standard 2.4 metre ceilings to somewhere more generous in height. The height isn't the only neat thing about them – upstairs in the master bedroom, the architect created a beautiful folded ceiling, a bit like a butterfly.

Staircases are areas that often get ignored or underrated in a build or renovation but not so in this home. The staircase (see page 149) is simple and elegant but what elevates it from a utilitarian space to something beautiful in its own right is the space beside it creating a void occupied gently by beautiful glass Bocci lights sourced by the client prior to my engagement. The steel and timber structure, which leads up to the bedroom level, feels light and strong at the same time.

While there's a strength to the design of the house, that doesn't mean there's no room for a softer approach, as seen in the travertine and timber palette, with touches of brass, in the kitchen and bathrooms. That particular palette could have been designed just for me – my aesthetic and that of the client and architect are all beautifully aligned.

SPACE AND STORAGE

Allow me to spend a bit of time discussing space here. It really seems that in this house, most problems and challenges that any homeowner faces have been considered and solved. There's no need to squeeze anything into anywhere in this house. There are only a few things in life that strike me as truly luxurious, the main ones being time and space. Time to do what is most important to you – being with your family, creating something from nothing, building your dreams or whatever it might be. You miss it when you can't find the time, and should be truly grateful when you have it.

Space is at a premium in many of the homes I've worked on in my career, including some of my own, but in this one, as it's a new build designed by a clever architect, there is ample space in which to live as well as plenty of storage space.

Hallways eat up floor space, and a grand staircase is a luxury, but this home has considered the design importance of both. Both are generous in scale, and the hallway contains a wall of cupboards for everyday items from vases to platters. The kitchen has more than ample storage in both the main kitchen area and the butler's pantry. There's a kids' playroom with a wall of built-in storage that can be used for toys but also doubles as a robe should anyone plan to stay a little while. This area has its own bathroom, making it a true guest suite for anyone lucky enough to be invited to stay.

Moving up a level to the master bedroom suite, the bedhead takes up the whole of the back of the walk-through robe with hanging, shelving and drawer space flanking both sides leading into the ensuite bathroom. Bathrooms, too, all have storage solutions considered for elegant, everyday use.

The lounge room also has a discreet solution to TV/AV storage requirements. The wall, beautifully panelled in a Ralph Lauren woven wall covering, hides shelving, suitable for the CD or DVD collection, with audiovisual equipment hidden away inside the blackbutt-panelled cabinet below the television.

There are only a few things in life that strike me as truly luxurious, the main ones being time and space.

Left: The hallway between the formal and informal living spaces is lined with storage.

Opposite: In the informal living area, cupboards flanking the television push to open and provide ample storage.

THE LAYOUT

Everything I've written so far sounds like a love letter to the architect, and it is really. There was nothing for me to correct in this home; except for specifying the covering of the bedhead and lounge wall panelling, I was able to walk into a well-thought-out home with plenty of consideration given already to how this family would use the space.

Whether the owners enter the house through the garage or the front gate from the street, the first rooms they come to are the formal ones. The combined, open-plan adult spaces present the home at its most refined. As far as planning the layout goes, the decision to make the first interior space you see the formal one with its raked ceiling, massive proportions and elegantly placed low window and enormous glass doors was a brilliant one. The home presents beautifully at every angle, but placing this room prominently really shows the architecture at its best.

The kitchen sits between the two living and dining spaces, servicing both with ease. The family room also looks onto the pool area so parents can keep an eye on the goings-on from the kitchen or the lounge room.

The playroom is separated from the family space by the generous staircase, which means that noise can be contained in that space, and yet it's close enough that you can keep an ear out for when things go just that little bit too quiet. As any parent knows, there's nothing more unusual than children playing quietly – it usually signals that they're doing something they shouldn't, but in this layout the kids can have their own space, mess and all, while the rest of the home can be kept as pristine as a family home of three children can be.

As I've mentioned, the playroom also doubles as guest quarters – a neat retractable door separates the space when the occasion requires. There's a bathroom to service this area, a study between it and the hallway, and a powder room for guests located far enough away from entertaining spaces for privacy but close enough for convenience.

Upstairs, the master bedroom is at the front of the house, separated from the three children's rooms and bathrooms by the staircase. This gives the parents their own retreat with an area big enough to lounge in and read a book if they need to get away.

The greatest success of the layout is the way it solves all the challenges of everyday family life. Privacy and proximity, utility and amenity are so beautifully addressed in a massive home that still manages to feel quite intimate.

LIGHTING

I'm often brought into a house to try to improve its levels of lighting – either there aren't enough windows or they're in the wrong place, or the actual lighting fixtures are inappropriate or inadequate. I had no such problems here, and didn't even have to consider lighting at all. It was all decided before I was brought in.

On the natural front, literally every room has a window or huge door with an outlook onto something green and beautiful. As far as artificial lighting goes, the architect had avoided some of the normal interior designer go-tos in favour of a more discreet and subtle approach. You won't find a feature pendant over either dining table. The family dining table simply has three drops of very small diameter black cylinders, while there's no lighting at all over the adult dining table. Instead, candles and battery-operated table lighting of the sort you usually see in upmarket restaurants combine to create quite a moody ambience.

The ceilings were left intact – there were no downlights peppering their smooth white surface. Instead, white, quite industrial wall lights are used to amazing effect to light both the ceilings and artworks in the adult entertaining space. White wall sconces of a different kind also light up the walls in the family living space.

It's such a relief to walk into a home and not have to think about how to tidy up the Swiss cheese effect created by too many downlights. Wall sconces incidentally, out of fashion for years, are having a resurgence in contemporary interiors. They have many advantages – not only do they save the ceilings from interruption but they also serve as sculptural elements both in their form and in the way they spread light onto adjoining surfaces and objects.

There are no LED strip lights glowing underneath cabinets or overhead cupboards. There are no tricky hanging pendants over bedsides, no clusters of three feature lights used to fill voids. The lighting, while doing everything it needs to do in a functional sense, does not in any way interfere with the integrity of the building – and that's all due to the skill of the architect. This kind of 'function first' approach in such a beautifully pared-back and carefully detailed home suits the family perfectly. There's nothing fussy, nothing that gets in the way or that has to be handled carefully so as not to be damaged. There are only the things that a family needs, albeit in their purest and most thoughtfully designed form.

Opposite: Three simple black cylinders drop down above the dining area, leaving the ceilings otherwise clear of lighting.

Design elements

INSPIRATION

It's hard to know where inspiration comes from.
Sometimes I have an idea in my head that I would like
to use, but don't know when or where. With this home,
because of the brass detailing the architect had already used
in the door handles, hinges and other fixtures and fittings,
I knew that brass should come into play in some form or
another. The thing that was ticking away in the back of
my mind was how cool brass looks with navy blue velvet.
The effect, I thought, would be very luxurious. This was
probably the starting point for me, apart from the obvious
instruction the building seemed to give me to create
something unfussy, honest and honourable.

Scale was also an inspiration here. There aren't many
opportunities to use furniture the size that this home
requires. Both dining tables, for instance, had to be three
metres long to look right, and so would need to be custom
made. I had to think about who was up to such a task,
and came up with a few names of places I regularly go to.

These days I don't get much chance to visit
showrooms, but when I do, I mentally file ideas away for
later use. I also take lots of snaps and note interesting
details, and try my best to memorise where I see
something so I know where to find it again.

I saw an amazing dining table with the most elegantly
curved brass legs made by Australian designer Barbera at a
friend's store. This sprang to mind while walking through
with my clients on my first visit to the house. It's fortunate
that when the right time comes, the right objects tend to
bubble to the surface of my memory.

Below: The winter magnolia was relocated from elsewhere on the block to be the central focus of the living spaces.

I was slowly starting to build an idea of what might look right for this home just by thinking and listening. There's nothing wrong though, if for you, that inspiration comes from reading magazines, books, surfing the web or tearing out pictures from catalogues. Whatever it is that interests and excites you is fair game, so keeping this stuff together either electronically or physically is the key. I do it mostly by memory and then source on the web but your inspiration might not be quite as easy to access as my imagination is for me. It's good to have a bible of things you like to refer back to so you can make good decisions.

Inspiration also comes in the feeling I get about clients. I usually know what they will, or won't, like. That comes from talking to them, observing them and listening to what they say and how they say it. I also try and get some images from my clients on first meetings so I can see if I'm right.

In this instance I was taken by a few unexpected details from my client's reference. There was a bit of mid-century Danish furniture there, and while the house has a quite understated feel in the same way that American mid-century furniture does, it also has that sophistication you see in modern Japanese furniture and architecture. I expected to see that simple and functional yet effortlessly beautiful form come through in the design reference. The architecture seemed to indicate clean lines and contemporary design; by talking to my clients I discovered it was the mood of the picture that they were trying to convey rather than the actual pieces of furniture. This is something you need to consider, too, when gathering up your own reference.

Scale was also an inspiration here. There aren't many opportunities to use furniture the size that this home requires.

Right: The artwork and architecture are completely in harmony in this home.

Opposite: Organic forms and brass details add interest and colour to the coffee table in the formal lounge room.

Complementing the artwork in the room, the soft pink rug provides contrast to the occasional tables in the master bedroom.

Some thoughts
on reference

When you find images of things you like, think about why
you like them. Is it the colour, texture or form? Do you like
the scale? Or is it the way the room has been put together
with lots of elements or with very few? Think about what
you find appealing in those pictures; it could be that the
overall feeling of a picture is right, even though you don't
like the separate pieces. It could also be that you love a
particular chair in a pic but the general look of the image
doesn't match what you're after. The important thing is to
understand why you are pulling out the particular pieces
of reference; perhaps including a few notes with them to
help remind yourself later could be a good idea.

   I rarely actively observe what other designers are doing.
I do, though, love to look at magazines and books, so it's
more information by osmosis. The bits and pieces tend to
coalesce into something when the right brief comes along.
It is hard though to say that any idea or creation is truly
original. There are plenty of people and places that inform
my style just as there will be for you when creating yours.
The trick is to keep your eyes open everywhere you go and
take note of what appeals to you and try to figure out why.

   Patterns, combinations and textures all need to be
noted when you're viewing something you like. You can
appreciate an object at first glance, but it's by really
observing your reference that you create better spaces. I did
this when I started out and still walk into new spaces like
hotels or restaurants and quietly disassemble the individual
pieces in my mind. It gets quite distracting at times but is
just one of the hazards of the job, I guess.

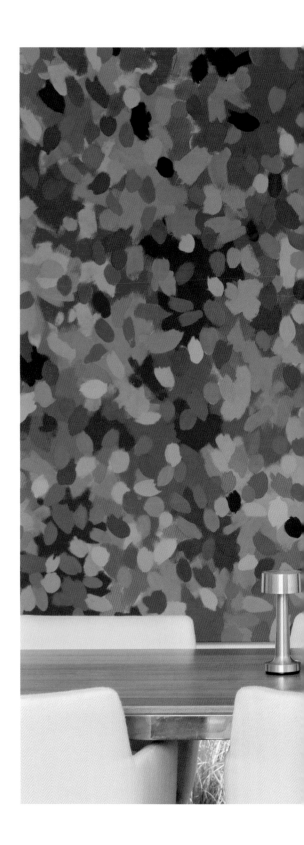

Below: Subtle hints of luxury can be seen in the brass detailing of the table.

Opposite: Not something that
you would necessarily register,
but the similar forms of the
various furniture legs help
create a sense of coherence.

Furniture choices

I live a life not driven by appearances but of comfort and
practicality. Yes, the result is sophisticated, but I understand
what it is to live with small children. That means robust and
resilient furniture, comfortable yet practical fabric choices,
washable or non-fussy elements not so delicate or so
precious that you lose sight of what is really important in
your home – the relationship with your family. Give me
a happy home over a tidy, perfect one any day of the week.

In terms of furnishing this home, these people live
firmly in reality, and were able to decide very easily where
to spend money wisely and where to be more moderate.
Looking at the project, I'm sure you wouldn't know the
big ticket items from the more modest; the whole scheme
flows beautifully from lush to practical, from everyday to
special occasion.

The first living/dining space you encounter is so big
that it needs oversized furniture. This amount of space
allows you a certain freedom, but also constraint. Freedom
in the way you can really go bananas with the number of
pieces, zoning it in any way you see fit that will suit the
house and the family who live in it. Constraint sets in
though in the size of the furniture; there's no use buying
a 1.8-metre-long table for such a huge room. Even though
some furniture was adapted from product that was readily
available as part of a retail range, every piece was made
from scratch to fit the size of the rooms.

The sourcing process was the same as always; I visited
showrooms with my clients to see what they liked. I
scoured websites to show them the sort of forms I was

thinking about. This project had the luxury of time, and
the owners saw the value in investing in pieces of furniture
that would stand the test of time and age well; that meant
bespoke furniture was a must.

TABLES AND CHAIRS

I've already mentioned the Barbera table, which was one
of the pivotal pieces of the design puzzle. I saw the round
version of it in my friend's showroom and fell for it. The
metal legs (brass on the one I loved) curve gently at the top
but have a nice straight line otherwise, making the piece
look both soft and strong. The top on the retail version was
marble, which wasn't right here because of the mass of
travertine flooring throughout the living spaces. As
blackbutt and brass were used so well in the architecture,
we decided that the palette should be reflected in the
furniture. We had a table shape; the size of it was dictated
by the space, while the materiality was informed by the
building. I just had to brief the maker. Once that was done,
chairs with a slightly curved and tapered leg were found
that worked with the table. These were upholstered in a
subtle white-on-white chevron pattern, which was just
right for the house.

The other dining room needed a table too, but we
couldn't just replicate the first one, mainly because it was
quite an investment and not of the type of material you'd
use every day. The family dining room table is more robust
but still a thing of subtle beauty. Another tapered leg came

into play, again based on the retail version of a supplier's table. This time, though, the leg is the timber element, also custom made in blackbutt to work in perfectly with the house. The top is of Corian, 12 mm thick and perfectly flat and white. The table, if marked and worn, could be returned to good condition simply by scouring with abrasive cleaner or a quick buff with some lambswool.

Everyday use and general wear and tear were also a factor with the dining chairs. We chose a white plastic one, so that parents and children can all relax and enjoy family time together without worrying about the furniture. This is the real success of designing a home for a family – you allow them to simply live their lives. They can focus on their relationships because they don't need to be fussed by *things*. This is the true gift of a well designed home.

THE LIVING AREAS

Still on the family, more informal, side, the sofa needed to comfortably accommodate five. As you know, we were spoilt for space in this house and floated a number of variations of massive couches, chaise longues, ottomans and single occasional chairs, but the version that the clients felt most at home with and thought would suit their way of interacting in the space was a massive U-shaped sofa with a chaise longue on each side, allowing the family any number of ways to lie down and enjoy TV time together.

To make lying down more accessible to everyone in the family, we went with a large, studded leather ottoman instead of a coffee table. It can be used with a tray to rest drinks on, left soft to rest your feet on or brought closer to the sofa to be something to lie on. This versatility is what is required from a hard-working family home. Another consideration with the ottoman vs coffee table decision was that there were no hard edges or sharp corners that could hurt the smallest child, or anyone else for that matter, should they run foul of the furniture. An interesting detail to note is in the sofa, which was made by the same manufacturer as the informal dining table that sits next to it. The sofa legs are blackbutt and we had those legs custom made to reflect the shape and taper of the dining table legs. These details are important when you're creating a high-end home; you may only register them subconsciously but the space will feel more complete to you.

Back to the formal living area – the sofas are blue velvet with the same Barbera-designed brass legs as the table, albeit on a smaller scale. Again, it was important to pay attention to this kind of detail, especially as the sofas and dining table are so close together. The sofas themselves, which face each other, are very structured looking and sculptural, with no loose cushions.

The coffee tables have a more traditional pattern with a parquetry top and, again, pick up the brass detailing of the other furniture and of the building itself. As one table wasn't big enough to fill the space, a pair were used, side by side. Two console tables were also sourced to sit behind the sofas so that we had somewhere to style in some height and interest, and also heighten the visual level of the room by placing a lamp on a taller table. That variation in height gives the room a sense of movement, and allows the eye to roam around and take in different levels and layers.

THE MASTER BEDROOM

The formal dining table also influenced the design of the bed in the master bedroom; the legs, again, reflect the taper on the brass legs downstairs. The bed is a fusion of blackbutt and brass that sits against a textured bedhead wall.

The sitting area in the master bedroom also has ample space to fit a sofa but we decided that two single chairs were all that were needed, as there would never be more than two in the room. Another brass element can be seen in the teardrop-shaped occasional cocktail tables, clustered together. Visual height was achieved in the corner by placing a rather large and beautiful lamp on a marble-topped table. I know I said earlier that marble had no place in this project because of the floors, but the floors in the master bedroom are a chunky pebble kind of carpet which tied in well with the colour and texture of the marble of the table.

OUTDOORS

Moving outside, practicality and scale also dictated the choice of the outdoor dining setting, a lazy Susan finding its way into the middle of the metal and glass eight-seat dining table. If you used such a thing inside, it might be questionable, but outside it is pure brilliance. It's interesting how rules that apply in one area won't be the same in another. Design fundamentals stay the same, but successful use of elements in different spaces really depends on where they appear and in what intensity and form.

Opposite: Short of having a table custom made, one of the right size can be formed by putting two together.

Opposite: The table, an over-scaled piece of furniture, looks perfectly in scale in the enormous room.

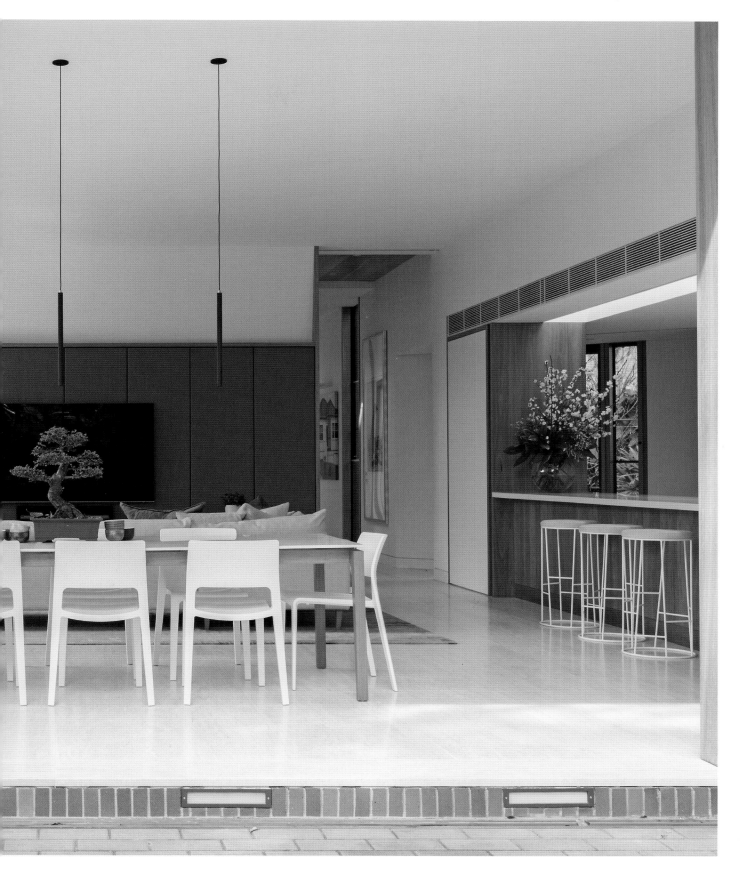

Opposite: The home was designed around the winter magnolia, which also formed the basis of most of the decorating choices.

Colour

USING A TREE AS A STARTING POINT

Before they built this new home, the clients already had a house on the block, in a different position, but one standout feature they were passionate about keeping was a winter magnolia tree that flowered around the time of their daughter's birthday.

The architect, builder and landscaper worked with the client to relocate the tree to its new location and built the house so it could be seen from the living spaces and master bedroom, such was its appeal for only a few weeks a year. The branches, devoid of leaves, burst to life with deep purple flowers, and it's easy to understand why you would go to such effort to build a home around a tree.

The house itself doesn't have much in the way of colour, with brick, blackbutt, brass and travertine being the material palette. The architect specified white paint in every room, so opportunities to bring in colour, in the same way the garden has in that short period where the flowers burst to life, were few and far between. There are no feature walls or small rooms to treat with textured wallpapers or contrasting paints. The house was so much the architect's vision, it seemed obscene to taint it with anything but the purity the clients and architect had agreed upon.

That meant that colour had to come from inclusions. Rugs, sofas, occasional chairs, art and décor are the pieces that allow for a break from the pared-back palette.

Blue velvet in the sofas works in with a mottled grey and silver rug in the formal lounge space. One artwork in the room picks up the colour of the magnolia flowers; another works with the mood of the building and the sculptural feeling of the tree. The decorative elements and floral arrangement link the pieces together, and add another burst of colour. This room and, indeed, the whole house could have been pared back, but the clients engaged me because they wanted an interior that felt quite homely.

The only colour in the informal space comes from the blue almost camouflage pattern rug that spans the large area under the U-shaped sofa. Décor elements tie in with the rug and there is also a floral arrangement that relates to the Chinese woman featured in the artwork in the formal living room. These simple cues work well from space to space, helping to integrate elements across the home.

Upstairs in the master bedroom the colour comes from the pinkish linen on the bed; this ties in with the mauve linen chairs in the relaxation area. Artwork again is the inspiration for the colour in the space, the sole picture being one the clients already owned.

The rug was the only other decorative element, bringing together the other elements in the space as well as giving a base for the lounging corner of the room. The pattern of the rug ties in nicely with the blue camouflage rug in the informal lounge room.

Throughout the house, there is art that the clients sourced during our consultation period as well as after the installation of their furniture. When I came back, there were even more pieces, and they all work well with what was already there. I love art, but find it best to encourage clients to find their own, so they can add in a layer that is not only colourful and interesting but meaningful to them.

Opposite: With three walls of windows looking onto the garden, the sitting area in the master bedroom is an ideal parents' retreat.

Adding an extra layer

Looking over the whole project the palette was exceedingly simple: brass and blackbutt featured throughout, then woven natural materials, a touch of blue velvet and an even smaller amount of tan leather and mauve and we're done. This simple palette managed to bring all the elements and all the rooms together.

Woven wall coverings introduce an interesting texture to the informal lounge room wall and the bedhead wall in the master suite. A durable, almost fine rattan-like woven material was used for practicality in both spaces while the flat colour and uniform texture fit in well with the bricks with their repeated geometric pattern.

That's the thing with choosing textures and materials. You need to look for inspiration in the environment. It might be the bricks, it might be the colour of the earth outside, it could be an amazing tree in the garden or the most random thing. If you really pay attention to where you are and what you're working with, you may find you choose things that, in retrospect, look very deliberate but may in fact just be well-informed, happy coincidences.

DECORATION

All homes come to life with the final layer of decoration. More than anything, it can tell a story of the home and the people who live there.

The master bedroom, the most private area of the whole house, is quite sparse in terms of decoration. The coffee tables and lamp give the lustre that only a metal such

Below: The sheer scale of the room is only obvious when you see how dwarfed I am by it.

as brass can, while a simple bonsai tree fits the home's Japanese mood, and relates to the treetops seen from the windows on three sides of the room.

Books, décor pieces and candles were used sparingly on the corner and bedside tables, with the only other decoration coming in the form of the bed linen, in its shades of soft pinks, slate grey and wheat. A succulent adds that last pop of life to the room.

The informal lounge, being a full tilt family space made for all the hubbub of everyday life, is devoid of most traditional décor. There are the obligatory vessels to tie in the blues of the rug and the browns of the timber; a few large candles occupying a corner next to the built-in lounge cabinets lined with the textured Ralph Lauren woven covering, but apart from the cushions strewn fairly randomly across the massive family couch, there isn't much more to speak of in terms of accoutrement.

The family dining table has a lovely sculpture, sourced by the owners on completion of the home, standing guard at the end and, save for another substantial bonsai and a few Japanese tea cups, that's it for décor too.

Not so in the formal living area. It's the area where, when the kids are watching a DVD on the massive couch in the adjoining room, the adults can converse in quite a refined space. The coffee table is heavily decorated. There are books and candles, natural elements, décor items, *more* candles, some coasters and almost every sensible thing a good coffee table needs.

As I mentioned before, the floral arrangement, obviously something with a limited life span, fits in well with the artwork. The dining table is sparsely adorned, needing only a few light sources in the form of battery-operated brass table lamps and some geometric candles.

That's quite the idea of decoration. It's to tell a story of how each space is used and to reflect the tastes and desires of the occupants, but also to tie together potentially disparate elements and give a cohesive look that, otherwise, may not be achievable. I know that sounds like a massively grand and important statement about something that can be seen as frivolous, but the truth is the truth. When you use decoration well, you are able to unify your design and the visual result is far better for it.

The key is to look for commonality, then complement and contrast. In the formal lounge, the contrasting elements are the more detailed ones like coral or the agate coasters and trivet. Even the more rustic timber texture contrasts with the other super-refined timber textures.

Complement comes in the form of the floral arrangement's colour and pattern, which works perfectly with the painting. The form of the blue sofas has a subtle curve to the arms and legs that ties in with the curve of the table and chairs. The light on the table, too, has the same curve and is of the same material. Introducing another metallic in the form of the silver bowls is a deliberate move to both provide contrast in the room and complement the gold hues of the brass.

It's a house in which detail is vital. In such a well-considered space, it is important to ensure that every element brought into it works. For me, it has been a rare opportunity to contribute to such a home, and I feel privileged to have been able to do so.

When you use decoration well, you are able to unify your design and the visual result is far better for it.

Opposite: Even the barnacles on the occasional table in the master bedroom echo the colours of the winter magnolia.

In a subtly dramatic room such as this, the artwork needs to be bold and eye-catching, but sympathetic to the space overall. The fireplace is in the divider between the living and dining areas.

Pieces of
the puzzle

——

CHILD'S PLAY

There is absolutely nothing wrong with having a kid's room just being a fun, raucous, playful space with no particular creative flair. Kids really only need to have the things they love, their favourite toys, their favourite colours and good, robust and functional furniture – the stylish bit generally doesn't concern them too much. Kids' rooms, though, can be places of pure creative freedom and fun in terms of colour, pattern, inclusions and design innovation.

There's no reason, either, why you can't create a child's room that feels like a part of the overall look of your home, either in keeping a similar style or by just giving it the same level of attention to detail and design.

Nurseries have to be the most exciting of all rooms to create. And also the oddest in some ways, because you're creating a room for someone you haven't yet met, although the idea of who they might be and what their little personality will be like is a wonderful thing to occupy your imagination. How your decorating scheme fits into all that is truly up to you – I've heard of jungle themes, pretty pastels, neutral or monochromatic and any number of creative applications to create baby's very first space.

If you want something sweet and girly, go for it, but if you want something peaceful and tranquil, you'd be well advised not to push the visual volume up too loud as you might run into issues when it comes to rock-a-bye baby to sleep. Interestingly, I've heard that if you put a baby in a yellow room, there's a fair chance you'll be in for a bout of crying. Blue, pink and lavender, however, are meant to be calming, and green is supposed to be tranquil – that's the idea, anyway. These are great things to know if you're spending one of your last weekends, sans baby, painting prior to your new arrival.

Nursery

To say there are myriad choices for children's décor would be a major understatement. As with all interior decisions, it's making the choices that are right for you and your home that is the major challenge, and constraints are, as always, your friend and guide.

Firstly, your child's gender may dictate a palette, although what that means for you is as subjective as what kind of music you like. Gender stereotypes of pink for girls and blue for boys are predictable and safe, but any pastel colour is going to be sweet for an infant's bedroom. The choice of colour or the choice of no colour at all is purely up to you. There are some very beautiful nursery images online of whites and neutrals or subtle grey on greys. For the best chance of restful sleep for everyone in the house, do think about making sure the room isn't too visually bright.

Think about adding in playful or whimsical elements for a sense of childlike fun. Wall decals are a brilliant way to add a cool, fun element to the room without the hassle of wallpapering. On top of that, they're one of the easiest ways to jazz up a wall, and are in many playful shapes and colours appropriate for kids' rooms. I've used these super cute watermelons to add a pop of colour and geometric pattern, but there are any number of choices from metallic to colourful objects.

Another great way to bring a whimsical element into the room is with something as simple as a mobile. Its colourful elements, reflective surfaces, felted bits and bobs or natural additions such as wooden beads or feathers will keep your little one amused as well as add visual interest to their room.

Rugs and soft furnishings play a part in infants' rooms just as they do in any other interior space. Starting with the baby linen, which is a pretty cute place to start, you can have fun mixing and matching the sheets and bumpers, and adding in a few decorative cushions for colour and texture. Colour and texture may well be teddy bear colour and snuggly texture but, hey, horses for courses.

Light is another important matter in nurseries. Firstly, make sure you can control the level of light in the room at any time. You will want to make it relatively dark during the day, so block-out blinds or drapes are a must, although you can layer in soft sheers for effect. You will also need a controlled level of light near the change table, either by having your room lights on a dimmer, or task lighting with a low voltage bulb.

You can create a sense of play with light by projecting stars or shapes onto the walls and ceiling. There are some cool kids' lights that play gentle music and rotate characters or shapes around the room.

As the major furniture element in the room, the crib obviously needs to be sturdy and comfortable but can also be interesting, cool and fun. They come in a wide variety of shapes and forms, metallics and colours being in fashion right now, but a good tried-and-true classic white is as good an option as any for that timeless and adaptable look.

The other super important piece of furniture, aside from the change table, is the night-feeding chair. You'll need this to be as comfortable and comforting as possible for your sleep-deprived daze. This chair isn't just for night feeds either – you'll find yourself sitting in it during the day, waiting for your baby to fall asleep before you sneak out of the room, so make sure you can read a book on it if needs be as well rock the bubba. If it's beautiful and stylish, all the better, but seriously, trust me on this one, make sure it's comfortable. Easy to clean is another bonus, too, as babies do tend to leak.

Small child's room

The fun is just getting started when you get to upgrade your bub into their very own big boy or girl room. Our boy's room started out as a tiny space under the stairs that was painted in his favourite colour and covered in Spiderman decals and details, his favourite at the time.

I didn't have to spend more than a few hours to turn what used to be a study into his very own room, albeit small but, frankly, just the right size for a little guy. It doesn't take much to excite a small child either – just their favourite colour or colours, their favourite things represented in some way and their favourite belongings to play with, and they're sweet. The real fun comes when you try and see the world through their eyes and create a little place of wonder for them.

Turn your mind towards your child's favourite picture books; they're filled with places of surprise and adventure, so you can be confident that if you achieve the same thing for their room, they're going to be pretty happy with your efforts.

Colour and pattern are the perfect backdrop for kids' rooms. Paint applied in interesting ways by carving up different shapes on the walls might be a little too adventurous for some adults, but can be a really cool way to play with colour and shape for not a lot of expense. You can achieve even more detailed results

with wallpaper, though it does take some skill to hang. Decals can be changed semi-regularly for a few hundred dollars, and your kids can help you apply them, or even do it all on their own. It will give them a real sense of ownership and pride.

If you see the walls as the backdrop, think about what else you can put into the scene. It might be a timber tree bookshelf or a suspended bed tree house, a car-shaped bed or any number of theatrical inclusions that will light up your little one's mind. You can keep the room simpler and more chic, too, if you wish, but do always consider the personality and desires of your child and what *they* want from their space.

Kids will need a place to play as well as a place to store everything they play with, so boxes to dump toys in are a great idea, as are shelves to get everything off the floor and on the walls in an ordered, or semi-ordered, fashion. By creating a place for everything to go, you're setting up your child with the best possible chance of keeping their room clean and tidy, and you happy.

Think, too, about the right flooring for your child, who'll spend time playing on the floor. A soft rug will save their knees but play dough, clay and sand don't come out of furry or shaggy rugs as easily as, say, a flat weave or cut pile rug. Variation of colour and pattern will help you live with mishaps and, as with all spaces, colour, texture and pattern in rug form are a great base for the room.

There also needs to be a place to do homework, crafts or just draw, so that means a desk. This will want to be as far away from a school desk as possible, though, to let their creativity shine, so think of colours or interesting shapes, and make sure they're size-appropriate for your child's age.

Artwork is important in every room in the house, but here, choose art with your kids or use some of their favourite school projects to decorate their walls. It could be fun to even blow up some of their art onto custom wallpaper and apply it at macro size. Anything that sparks their creativity is OK, and different kids will love different things, from Barbie or Batman to Lego, rainbows, sparkles or animals. Just find a way to work in what they love, and build the rest of your scheme around it.

Kid-sized furniture is a good idea too. I've used a modern take on a beanbag that can sit against something to be a seat or lie flat on the ground to play on or around. To dial up the cuteness in your kid's room, you can also find cool wingback armchairs or dining settings that have been reduced down to little people size. Sure, they'll outgrow them, but they'll also get too grown-up for the general playfulness of the room at about the same time, so you'll need to let their room evolve with them.

Young adult's room

Kids grow up way too quickly these days, so when I say 'young adult', I mean that stage after childhood that now includes tweens. Young people have particular tastes, as any parent finds when their children suddenly become disdainful of almost every single thing they have, say and do. It seems that this age is the quickest to adopt trends and adhere to them tightly, while also needing to have a feeling of individuality for themselves and their spaces.

For a young adult brief, you need to consult with the particular young adult in your life. Sit down and try to decipher, as best you can, the grunts and 'whatevs', and use some reference or get them to build a Pinterest page of what they and their peers think is cool.

Also consider what you think they'll need to live in their space. Shelving, storage and order is a brilliant thing to aim for. At least if *you* think about what they might need and how they might be able to keep themselves ordered, you might have a good chance of them doing the same.

While it might be a good idea to have a desk in their room to work at, also think about having a work area in a more communal area of your home, such as the kitchen or lounge area, so that you can keep one eye on their online life.

A standard theme for young ladies is the 'Kinfolk' look of whites and linens, fairy lights, bleached woods, feathers and beads. You might have a young hipster in your midst, though, who's into music, or yours could be of the sporting variety. The important thing is to not theme your young adult's room, but give them the things they think are cool, and focus on how they will live in their space, considering how much time this age group spends out of your view.

You can create amazing effects with wallpapers, full wall murals or creative paint treatments. One option is to paint diagonal sections on the walls, or two-tone it by having one colour at the top and ceiling with another from, say, two-thirds of the wall height down to the floor. The success or failure of these painted finishes really depends on the dimensions of the room you're applying them in. If in doubt, put masking tape lines on the wall and have a look at it before you paint. Worst case, if you or your young adult doesn't like the result, you can always paint over it, or better still get them to.

Young guys are way easier to please in terms of style. Generally speaking, most of them have yet to develop a sense of their own style, so it's a matter of giving them a cool, relaxed, unfussy and masculine space. If I think back to my teenage bedroom, it was pretty minimal and in a state of disorder most of the time. Accept this and your life will be that little bit easier.

Common elements for a masculine look are woods, dark colours and tones, tan leather and any fabrics that are relaxed and don't need much looking after. Think cottons and crumpled linens. Denim, tan leather and heavy open weaves are all good accents for this unfussy and unfussed look.

You might want to include a good chair or couch if space permits, and shelving to stack whatever it is they're into at the time. Cupboards and drawers allow for some sense of order. Considering how long teenagers need to sleep, it's wise to invest in the best bed you can afford. Also, make sure they can filter out light effectively with either drapes or block-out blinds. Sure, you'll have trouble getting them out of bed by midday, although you can always use electric block-out blinds and keep the remote yourself!

Getting your young adult involved in the creation of their own space will help give them a sense of responsibility for it. That's the idea anyway – good luck with it in reality.

Character-filled house

COMFORTABLE HOME FOR A FAMILY

The brief

Years ago, we wanted to trade up from our North Bondi apartment in Sydney to a house in the same area. Looking for such a place was an eye opener, let me tell you. At the time, our budget could have bought a two-bedroom, semi-detached knockdown with the most diabolical bathroom and kitchen combination. It's hard to believe that someone actually *lived* in it prior to it going on the market. To say we were disheartened would be an understatement.

We happened to be visiting some friends in Edgecliff, at the city end of Sydney's eastern suburbs. It has the distinction of having both a train line and main road running through it, and is not a place we'd ever thought of looking. It felt so suburban.

Chatting to our friends, the discussion turned to the property market and the problems we had trying to manage the divide between our desires and our budget. Something about champagne and beer comes to mind. Our friends mentioned that the lovely couple across the road from them were thinking about selling, off market at that stage, but were seriously interested in upping stumps.

We were slightly curious about the house and finding out what it was worth, and to see whether or not we could embrace suburban life, albeit the inner eastern Sydney,

right next to the CBD suburban life that it was. So we organised to pay a visit. As soon as we walked in the front door we were hooked.

There were clearly problems with the house, but I knew it could work for our family. It was basically sound, and had some lovely Federation period details, but had also suffered from an unfortunate renovation in the '80s, with a nasty addition on the back, containing kitchen, bathroom and laundry.

I needed to reorganise some of the rooms to bring light into the centre of the house and to make them work more efficiently and logically. The main bedroom upstairs was also very open to the rest of the house — fine for a couple, not so good for a family. The house also needed a general smartening up and a bit of love to make it feel more contemporary and, as with many places, it was in desperate need of more storage. And then there was the courtyard, which was less than inspiring. We had a limited budget and not too much time — I wanted to do all the work without spending heaps of money or having to apply to council for a development application.

Opposite: Formerly part of one large room divided in half, the front sitting room functions as a winter lounge, complete with gas fireplace.

Right: Panelled walls and a black handrail were all it took to breathe new life into the staircase.

Structure

OUR INITIAL IMPRESSION

From the entrance, a staircase with lovely heritage-looking banisters created a void between the ground and first floors. The Federation façade was maintained in the front part of the home through ornate plaster ceilings, original skirtings and architraves, and beautiful coloured-glass windows looking onto jacaranda trees waiting to burst into bloom.

There were two fireplaces, a gas one for convenience and a wood or coal-burning one for the olfactory experience. The rooms were generous. And then we walked into the back of the house. The ramshackle bathroom and laundry and beige kitchen with glittering peach granite were quite an assault to the senses.

The courtyard was cut off from the living areas by the bathroom and laundry, meaning there was no sense of flow between indoors and out. Plus it was dull and ugly with printed concrete 'pavers' and no room for furniture, or to entertain in any meaningful way. It was also hemmed in on both sides by the neighbours' houses and a three-metre-high retaining wall only metres from the house. Beyond the wall was a terraced area accessed by a spiral staircase and, beyond that, a lovely well-cared-for green garden.

So we had some good and some bad. There was a glass atrium off the kitchen with some gaudy stained-glass windows, but a pretty bay window design. Glass panels in the ceiling led your eye out to the skyline and trees above.

Upstairs, the cunning owners had opened up the windows and back door to the terrace, letting light stream in and showing off the leafy outlook on all sides. Stick a fork in me because we're done.

We went back to our mates' house trying to keep our poker faces on until we got in their front door, and then let out our excitement. This was our new home.

But first there was the dance of how much to pay and how we were going to fill in the gap between asking price and our budget, but we managed to work it out swiftly. The little freestanding Federation cottage on a fair bit of land in a little cul-de-sac was ours. We were moving into my very first house as a homeowner.

PROBLEMS AND SOLUTIONS

The works I decided to do on the place were based on two things: time and money. That meant no long development application process or huge building costs involved in demolishing and rebuilding. Also, the house is in a heritage area so, while it's not heritage listed, it is in an area in which the council places value on façades. A complying development certificate (CDC) was the way to go, although its constraints were considerable. (You'll need to check local council requirements to see what is possible in your area.) In this instance, I could only work within the existing footprint and had to retain everything that was on the façade or connected to it. Changes to the two side walls, then, were out of the question, although replacing windows with some of the same size was no problem.

This meant I had to get creative about repurposing existing spaces within the home to give up their old roles and take on new ones.

What works for one family
doesn't necessarily work for
the next, and each set of
owners will change the house
to best suit themselves.

REWORKING THE INTERIOR

With the bathroom being in the wrong spot, the obvious place to put the new one was in our son's then bedroom, a long and relatively narrow room tucked under the stairs. It was the perfect spot to service the new bedroom, which I was going to create by carving up one big room that had been converted from two in an earlier renovation. What works for one family doesn't necessarily work for the next, and each set of owners will change the house to best suit themselves. This is as true for the previous homeowners' incarnation of the layout as it was for our need to adjust it.

The other part of the big room could then become another sitting room, a cosy winter room with a gas fireplace and a balcony overlooking the street. I had a vision of two old people in rocking chairs watching the goings-on in the street – but we are a good many decades away from that and, let's face it, my track record for staying in homes for too long is not so great.

The kitchen served us well in terms of its size and amenity, but was stuck in the past in terms of layout and finishes. The window was set in the side of the house so couldn't be touched, meaning it was a constraint to be worked around. The rest of the kitchen was up for grabs; it could change shape, change location and change its look to be more in line with the vision I had for the rest of the

home. The atrium, however, also had to stay, otherwise we would be in breach of the requirement of the CDC to retain the existing footprint. Another good constraint to consider in the design process.

Upstairs, the master suite was big and bright and lovely but, as I mentioned earlier, also had a mezzanine feel as there was no wall between it and the staircase. The walk-in robe was a bit dire as it was tucked under the incline of the roof and made from elements pieced together from the hardware store. It functioned but wasn't particularly lovely or easy to interact with.

The ensuite bathroom was the epitome of potential if I've ever seen it. It wasn't huge, and had soft apricot tiles and an apricot spa bath which you got into via a set of slippery steps. The hot water took ages to get to the taps, which were so temperamental that you could easily be having a scalding hot shower one second and a freezing cold one the next with only a millimetre of adjustment between the two. A veritable no-go zone, in other words.

The terrace, visible from the bathroom window, was unwelcoming at best. While the previous owners had lived in the house, they had looked after it and it was a great garden area, but we had let it become overgrown.

Opposite: With a cosy winter sitting room at the front, the house gradually opens up as you move towards the back.

197

A MATTER OF LIGHT

Everywhere we looked on that first inspection, I could see potential. Interestingly, the first inspection was the only one, as we fell so fast and so hard we knew straightaway that we needed to live there. During that visit, it shifted in no time from being the then-owners' house to ours.

I have bought a few properties in my time and the only one that didn't make me a profit was the one I bought with numbers in mind. The others were bought because I fell for them, seeing potential where others saw only hard work.

One of the main things to contend with in this house were the light levels, which went from one extreme to the other. Upstairs, light flooded in through the front windows, the dormer window, the glass door to the balcony and the bathroom window. Light and bright, the whole space was lovely to be in all year round.

Downstairs was a different story. The kitchen, with its bay windows and atrium looking onto the north-facing courtyard, was always awash with light – plus there was also the courtyard wall that reflected light into the room. But it was a different matter with the middle sitting room, which was cut off from the courtyard, the main source of light, by the bathroom. Even in summer, when light is at its strongest, barely any made it into the middle of the house.

The bathroom wasn't just obstructing the flow of light to the centre of the house, but it also opened right onto the courtyard, which could be pretty awkward if you were entertaining guests outside. Part of the solution involved tearing out the bathroom and laundry, and removing the wall to the middle lounge room. Using Velux skylights, which can be opened to let out heat and which have blinds to help with privacy and light control, was another. The last step to flooding the centre of the house with light was to replace the rear window with a wall of bifold doors that concertina back against the atrium door. This solution also connected the rear courtyard to the dining room, kitchen and lounge, which made a huge difference to the house.

REFLECTIONS ON A WALL

The view from the new dining room left a lot to be desired. Who wants to open up a wall to reveal another, higher, uglier one? That's what was waiting in the courtyard, a big three-metre-high, rough concrete retaining wall with flaking paint and no redeeming features. The wall also had three concrete pillars built into its structure that, one would assume, help stop the neighbours above from sliding down into the kitchen one wet day.

The wall was an issue, although it did reflect light into the back of the house. Reflection ended up being the solution. As we should all know by now, when you have a tight space, mirror gives the illusion of space. A few years ago, I started noticing ways that different people in my life had used mirror to great effect.

My professional mentor used mirror in a harbourside apartment to get views where there were none, and some friends with a courtyard no bigger than ours also mirrored a full wall of it, effectively doubling the perception of space.

So we have a big ugly wall, fairly ordinary pillars and a visually tight squeeze. Obviously the answer was mirrors, with large panels of the stuff going between newly stone-clad pillars. The mirrors, which reflect both the pillars and the lovely white shingle cladding of the house's exterior walls, give the whole space a really elegant and dignified look, and a sense of depth from inside and out.

Opposite: Mirror behind the chairs, not often used outside, cleverly adds to the feeling of space in the courtyard and helps blur the boundary between indoors and outdoors.

Opposite: A tidy take on a laundry, this nook is a tight squeeze but still manages to incorporate everything a family needs, even giving access to the clothesline outside.

These small design victories are always a buzz, and this was no exception. I probably even did a little dance.

SQUEEZING THE MOST INTO YOUR SPACE

We tackled the bathroom relocation challenge with relative ease, but there was still the problem of where to put the laundry. I tried working it into the kitchen, thought about integrating it into the bathroom and then started to panic a little bit.

I had a chat with a friend of mine, also a designer and a mum of young kids, and she mentioned if she was buying a house, it had to have a decent laundry. That meant some space allocated to it so it was big enough to use.

Darn it. I know it's necessary to have a laundry, especially for a house, but for so long I had been in apartments where I'd squeezed them into cupboards and kitchens and any other place that made sense in terms of access to floor wastes and plumbing points. I'd never really thought about how to make a laundry for myself.

There was, however, a weird little corner off the middle lounge room that had a door to the backyard. From the time I'd started designing the house, I had no idea what to do with it.

Cue Edison bulb.

If I could make a laundry out of the space, I'd be killing two birds with one stone. A little jigging and imagining and, sure enough, I was able to create a tight – yes, tight would be generous – but workable and functioning laundry with access to the clothesline area. These small design victories are always a buzz, and this was no exception. I probably even did a little dance.

BEDROOM STORAGE

Upstairs the 'walk-in' robe was more like a 'hunch your shoulders and squeeze yourself in sideways and mind your head' robe. Attic spaces are a great opportunity for getting that bit extra out of your house, ours having a small room, inside the walk-in, under the lowest point to keep bits and pieces like redundant baby strollers. The robe was a valuable space, but not suitable for everyday use for two people.

Refitting it with a simple flat-pack off-the-shelf system that housed shelves and baskets, hanging and hooks really elevated its functionality. Creating another robe on the other side of the room, adjacent to the exterior door, helped relieve it of some of its duties. We added in a row of three chests of drawers which allowed the new robe addition to be used as hanging space, while all the smalls and T-shirts were easily accessible in the shelves under the dormer window facing the street. This simple solution made sense of strange kinks in the dimensions of the room where the dormer window stuck out or the roofline sloped. I love a solution that solves a few problems at once, as this one did. When I realised it would work, I may well have done a second dance.

THE UPSTAIRS BATHROOM

When it comes to squeezing more into a space, the ensuite bathroom upstairs has to be a serious contender for some credit on how to get lots of amenity into a tiny room. Our three dogs need a bath, so does our son, not to mention my occasional love of a good soak – we needed a bathtub.

The downstairs bathroom was the wrong length for a shower and bath unless I put one in the other, which would not have been in keeping with the aesthetic of this home. The only way to include one, apart from locating it out on the balcony, was to put it in the ensuite.

The ensuite had room for a double-basined vanity, also bought off the rack online for a great price, a set of two showerheads, and all the normal accessories required for a bathroom to work day to day. With storage at face level, storage built into the vanity and even underfloor heating, this little

bathroom was like the Tardis, seeming far bigger once you stepped inside it than it did from the outside.

The ground floor bathroom had a few tricks up its sleeve, too. The inclusions were a reflection of those upstairs, the vanity and mirrored shaving cabinets a variation on the same type of product. The bit extra in this room comes in the form of a newly created cupboard under the stairs for overflow storage of towels, the vacuum cleaner and bulk toilet paper buys from when sixteen rolls were unbelievably cheap. Perhaps that was just me.

Left: Store-bought shaving cabinets sit above an off-the-shelf vanity unit, illustrating that low cost can still look good.

Opposite: With a young family and dogs, a bathtub is a necessity. The hand-held showerhead is the perfect tapware accessory.

Opposite: The breakfast bar was a way of making sense of the old atrium – and does happen to feature perhaps the best light in the house.

The reno was waiting to start, but I needed to crack the kitchen design to be able to brief the builders on plumbing and electrical points.

THE IMPORTANCE OF THE KITCHEN

Kitchens sell houses. That's the real estate gospel that has been adjusted recently to 'Kitchens and bathrooms sell houses.' The reason is that they're expensive, and when they're terrible they make the house feel terrible. On the other hand, when they're beautiful, functional, well designed and comfortable, the house feels that way too. They're expensive to replace when they're done wrong and a massive gift when done well.

Before I realised that council requirements meant I couldn't move the kitchen window, I had designed a cracking kitchen with butler's pantry, big island bench and all the modern inclusions that you'd want. I'd had it quoted and check measured, but unfortunately for me it wouldn't work unless I changed the window.

It was back to the drawing board – several times.

The interesting thing about design, and perhaps anything, is that the more you succeed, the more confident you become in your ability to succeed. The more you fail, the more you think you'll fail. In my mind I was failing. I wanted to create the perfect kitchen to suit the house, one that would function as a family kitchen and work with the atrium without blowing the budget.

Time was ticking along, and I was really feeling the pressure to deliver. The reno was waiting to start, but I needed to crack the kitchen design to be able to brief the builders on plumbing and electrical points. I even showed a very talented designer friend, thinking she could help. Just having someone to share the problem with generally works, but in this instance it didn't.

Fortunately for me, at the last minute I was able to find a simple galley kitchen solution with 900 mm deep benches (50 per cent deeper than usual) to help bring the benchtops closer together, and therefore make them a workable distance apart. I created two sets of three big wide drawers, overhead cabinets that were twice as deep as normal, and finishes and inclusions that functioned perfectly and were a little bit luxurious to boot.

The appliances are integrated, so there are no visible signs of modern technology that might throw off the classic heritage look I was aiming for. Exposed fridges and dishwashers are a bit clunky, so you're usually better off to hide them away and streamline the look of your kitchen.

The overhead cabinets are glazed with diamond wire safety glass (see page 210), which might remind some people of schooldays; it's the glass they used to use in fire doors. I love the look of it as it feels old but is also a little bit different from the fluted glass I'd used in the bathroom window upstairs. Both these materials are interesting options for a contemporary, classic heritage look, but the diamond wire glass is a little bit more edgy, which I felt the kitchen needed as everything else was so simple, grey and white. The shaker door profile is also a lovely detail to add to the cabinetry, as is the grey grout with the white tiles.

Opposite: Colonial bars on the windows add a lovely detail. The window seat is suspended above the floor to increase visual space.

Design elements

INSPIRATION

As a professional designer, the benefit of renovating your own property is that you can spend time in it working out things like light and ideal layouts. You can daydream about what it might be one day and picture no end of permutations of solutions to your design challenges. You can also study the house itself, get to know the area, get to know your neighbours, see their houses and their solutions and learn more and more as time goes on.

Our friends across the road had redeveloped their home years before we moved into the street, keeping the façade but gutting the entire house. It added enormous value to the home with the only cost being the loss of the original period charm we fell in love with in our house.

That made it easy for me to decide to restore and adjust rather than to remove and replace. The most respectful thing to do was to bring a sense of charm and quaintness back to the house. The council constraints also meant keeping a number of the things I might otherwise have removed.

The front windows were Federation-style casement windows with coloured-glass inserts. The style was lovely for the façade but a little too colourful for the rear alterations, so I decided to do something you should only do at your own peril. I mixed periods in my renovation.

I know.

The colonial glass panels I wanted for the back of the house have a simpler line, with the same grid as the Federation windows, but in a more stylised form that suited the style I wanted for that area.

The aesthetic direction was simple, elegant and timeless in order to highlight the beautiful heritage features in a contemporary way. It's not uncommon to see colonial bars and brass being used in modern interiors, especially ones trying to create a connection to a refined bygone era, and that's precisely what I was wanting to do in Edgecliff.

Details from American homes, such as panelled walls and coffered ceilings, were on my mind during the design phase, and I was also inspired by some lovely restaurants and bars in the area. I thought about what would bring the house to life, what was needed to restore its beauty and also reflect the modern lifestyle we wanted to lead in it.

I had pictures of brass and aged brass, lots and lots of white detailing to create a play of light and shade, white paired with grey and concrete, but with period-influenced finishes such as Shaker-style cupboard fronts and subway tiles. These finishes and inclusions aren't Federation, so wouldn't be appropriate for a restoration project, but this wasn't a restoration. It was a reimagining of a beautiful old building to bring it respectfully into the 21st century.

I wanted to make the house comfortable and inviting, but not fussy, not uptight and constrained. I wanted the pieces of the home that were originally amazing to be amazing again with a little TLC. I hoped to create a scheme that sat beside it and looked comfortable, not super modern, not traditional either, but a blend of both in a contemporary way.

I screen-grabbed a few pictures along the way, including a backdrop behind a Facebook photo I could

show to the builder with an example of the staircase panelling. Then there were pictures of the beautiful floors I created for my client in their apartment up the road in Elizabeth Bay, and shots from the internet of vanities, tiles and a few other bits and pieces all gathered together in a fairly thin reference folder. All up, there would have been no more than ten pictures of small details. The overall look was in my imagination so I just had to document it in order to pass it over to the builders to create.

DOCUMENTING

Documenting this project was one of the smarter things I've done when renovating for myself. I hired someone else to do it. I *can* document and have spent years of my career drawing things to give to builders, council and joiners, demonstrating to them what I cook up in my kooky mind. The truth is, though, I loathe it. I find the documentation process tedious. You need to really focus attention on every detail, which is hard to muster when you're in the flow of creative thinking. I find it a really structured experience and, frankly, I'm far more organic in my approach.

Once the documentation was done and done to perfection, I was able to hand it over to the builders. My job prior to that handover was to source all the prime cost, or PC, items. (These are items that haven't been chosen when the contract's signed, and can include anything from light fittings to whitegoods.) I don't mind this part so much as it's just a matter of searching through websites to find things that suit my vision.

SOURCING

Before the renovation, I went to a warehouse sale and picked up a whole bunch of toilets, basins and sinks that I hoped to use in our beach house renovation. As things turned out, we ended up renovating our home instead, so I used a few of the toilets and cisterns in Edgecliff.

I set my heart on the aged brass tapware first. I fell for them about a year before we'd found Edgecliff and had them stored away in my mind bank waiting for the right time and project to use them.

I found the handles for the kitchen cabinets online on a website called Overstock.com. It's brilliant for things like handles and door furniture, but not so great for things that require plumbing or electrical as they're mostly certified for use in the US.

I had some grasscloth paper I wanted to use, so that was one of the first inclusions into the scheme. The tiles, too, were another big part of the initial design phase. I had my heart set on French pattern travertine, which is made up of tiles of different shapes and sizes. It's really cost effective, it's interesting and it's textured *and* patterned and a brilliant base to use both indoors and out without having to change the finish or size. This simple trick helps unify the floor areas into one visual block, and makes the whole space look as large as it possibly can.

I took all the samples and laid them out on the boardroom table in my office so I could start to see the overall look and feel of the house in front of me.

When you're a designer you know all the right ways to do things. You do them over and over again for clients to achieve predictable results as well as limiting your exposure to delays and warranty issues. When you're the client *and* designer, though, things tend to get a little more ad hoc.

Because I didn't have to approve anything, I did what I tell other people not to do. I'd sit down and buy things here and there, knowing it would all come together.

FURNISHING DIFFICULTIES

I had a few constraints in the build, the main one being the step up into the dining room from the lounge room. If I had all the money in the world, I could have levelled it out, but that would have meant either raising the floor level in the front of the house or reducing the level at the rear. If I didn't lower the floor level of the backyard, whenever it rained, a deluge would flood the house. To do that would have cost around $70,000, and that was a large chunk of the budget that I could spend on more beneficial things.

Opposite: Diamond wire glass is used to create period ambience in the double-depth overhead cabinets.

The step up from the lounge into the dining room left me with a bit of an issue. Where I had pulled out the wall between the two spaces there was now an open void. The wall opposite had two doorways in it, one into the entrance hall, the other into the front sitting room. That left only two walls to put a TV and a sofa facing each other.

The problem was, one of these free walls had a fireplace in the corner, which made it too short to put a sofa. You might think that's obviously the spot for the TV. But the other free wall is a walkway from the entrance into the dining room. To put a sofa right in a walkway is probably a no-go? Yep, correct.

I hope you're starting to see my problem. A big room with no logical place to put a couch. The only wall that would work would be the one that was removed, the one with the step up into the dining room. Surely it would be weird to look at the back of a couch from the dining room?

My solution was a configuration made up of two chaise longues placed end to end plus a single seat module. The chaise sections had no backs, which opened up the view from the lounge to the backyard, but also removed the issue of staring at the back of a sofa while eating your breakfast. This unconventional configuration created an open-sided three-metre-long sofa, which comfortably seats four or five people. As it was my primary furnishing concern, this was one of the first things I'd sourced, shortly after I'd locked in the layout. I bought it hoping that the project would take two months. It took six, and the company that made it for me was very understanding, and kindly hung onto it for all that time. I also had two sofas in my office that were to be used in the front room in Edgecliff eventually, and I ordered a few things here and there that also started turning up to my office. This added pressure to my deadline to get the house finished, not to mention the damage it was doing to my budget.

Below: With the wall removed, the best solution to link the two rooms is an unconventional sofa design with a low back on one side.

Opposite: A panelled wall hides the laundry, with push-to-open doors on the far left. A candlestick-inspired chandelier takes centre stage above the dining table.

Below: Hung at just the right height, the brass chain light can be enjoyed at eye level when you are on the stairs.

I wanted to make the house comfortable and inviting, but not fussy, not uptight and constrained.

LIGHTING

I found all the lighting – some sourced during work hours but other bits when I scrolled through websites at night. I just bought and bought and bought things that I knew would piece together.

The lighting, in fact, is one of my favourite aspects of the home. There are several different types from several different suppliers. The two front rooms have the same fitting with a cool metal frame surrounding the shade (see page 233); these worked really well with what I wanted to do with the black gloss handrail of the staircase. For the entrance, I found another black metal fitting that looks like a globe of the world with a white orb in the centre. It also plays in nicely with the black accent of the stairs and links in with the two front rooms.

The staircase light itself, I think, is the big star, with its aged brass chains cascading down and filling the void of the staircase. As you're walking up or down the stairs, it's something beautiful to take in from every angle.

The light in the middle lounge room is a nice cheap option I had made in an inverted pyramid shape to complement the more ornate light hanging above the dining table. The light hanging over the breakfast bar (see page 206) was chosen by Olivier and he was very proud of himself when he got to see the result. I told him it was the best light in the house, and perhaps it is.

The bathroom lights are all downlights. There are nice, simple white wall sconces in the dining and lounge rooms and master suite – these wash the walls in light, and add a bit more of a contemporary edge to the scheme.

Below: Flat-pack drawers, cut down to fit under the shutters, have also been customised with brass handles.

Opposite: The industrial light works well with the metal bed – a good-value flat-pack buy.

Some thoughts on buying wisely

The smart way to buy furniture is the way I preach – to list everything out, find it all, lock it in and know that it all works. I sourced some things for my own home from IKEA. You'd never think I'd be spruiking flat-pack furniture, but with considered design, not everything has to be expensive. A house full of designer furniture can look amazing, but so, too, can a home made up of things from all over. It can include pieces from wholesale stores, along with flat-pack furniture, a few luxuries and some lower cost inclusions.

The IKEA furniture is used in the bedrooms. The robe in the master suite, the wardrobe fitting in the walk-in robe under the roofline and the drawers under the windows are all flat pack, put together by my builder. I've done my fair share of following flat-pack instructions, and know that putting a dowel where there should be a screw can be disastrous, forcing you to backtrack and pull apart half your work, cursing yourself at the same time. I'll avoid that if I can, thanks.

The bed downstairs was also a flat-pack jobby, looking like my great-grandmother's metal bed. The bedside tables in that room were also flat packs but they look the business, the line of the leg and the constrained proportions all suiting the room perfectly. The bedside tables upstairs weren't flat pack, but were bought at a retailer that everyone has access to, a last-minute change because I wasn't satisfied with the ones I had already bought. Don't be afraid to alter your mind at the last minute; it's worth finding the right solution. You don't want to walk past it every day and think, 'I could have done better.'

Opposite: Wholesale and retail sit neatly side by side, with inclusions sourced far and wide from many different suppliers.

There's no one solution to a space, but when you find one that works best, you know it.

BEDROOM DETAILS

The downstairs bedroom was a pretty easy one to solve. Bed and bedside tables were sourced from the same place, and the robes were existing, needing only a coat of paint and some new knobs. A rug and bed linen finished the equation. The lovely plantation shutters give the room an extra bit of finesse, light control and privacy.

The upstairs bedroom was more of a challenge, but still straightforward. The builders cut down the legs of the drawers under the window so the plantation shutters could open. Again, I changed the handles on the drawers as well as the robes to lift them from the ordinary to something that worked perfectly with the aesthetic language of the house. Sometimes all you need to do to make a piece sing is to alter it slightly, whether that be, for instance, by shortening or changing the legs, and altering small details that make a big difference, such as handles or knobs.

The flooring in the upstairs bedroom was one of the things I locked in when I was planning the design. The sample made its way onto my boardroom table alongside the floor tiles, the wall tiles, the kitchen benchtop and the wallpaper. It's grey and black sisal in a herringbone pattern that suits the style of the house and works well with the herringbone patterned grey tile in the ensuite. With the tiling, I used a black grout, and that, again, ties in with the sisal. It's those simple things, tying in patterns and colours, that make the spaces feel unified. You can look for opportunities to do this for your own rooms, retrospectively working in with existing elements, or while you're planning your next project.

The bedside tables in the master bedroom have little studs around the perimeter that made me think of a bedhead I'd seen. I bought the bedhead at one of my favourite wholesalers while searching for pieces for another project. The bedside tables and bedhead, from two different suppliers, one wholesale and the other retail, share a common language and sit perfectly beside each other.

I was away when the furniture was being delivered, and had several team members in the house receiving things, unpacking them and putting them in place for me to come and finalise the next day. They sent me photos and I noticed they'd used the bedside lamps I intended for downstairs in the upstairs room. The lights were metal, industrial and on hinged arms and while, they would have been fine upstairs, when I changed them to the more elegant linen shaded numbers I'd planned all along, several of the team commented on how they softened the space.

There's no one solution to a space, but when you find the one that works best, you know it. It's the sum of the parts that makes a room work, and there are rules to abide by, but a lot of it is also just having a feel for what balances and creates harmony in the space. The industrial lights tipped the room out of balance towards a harder look; the linen shades and elegant metal bases restored that balance.

Grasscloth paper provides a lovely textural element in the upstairs bedroom, and works well with the sisal flooring.

The use of colour

USING WHITE AS A BASE

When the foreman in charge of the painting team arrived, he mentioned how glad he was to see the colours I'd chosen for the house, as they made it simpler and quicker to paint. Almost all white. With white ceilings, white walls, white skirtings and white architraves, the whole project was pretty much one neutral, warm grey white called Whitsunday Island.

I chose quicker and simpler not because I'm lazy but because it also means cheaper. I had a finite budget and wanted it to stretch as far as possible, so I made it as easy on the builders and tradespeople as I possibly could.

That did, however, leave me with a relatively bland canvas. A white house with white walls and white woodwork doesn't leave many other opportunities for colour. I painted the front bedroom a colour called Palmer, partly because it is a lovely duck egg hue that I thought would be a nice point of difference to the white house, and partly because it had my name and I thought that would be cool.

The other colour of note, apart from the black used for the handrail of the staircase, is a lovely metallic gun metal grey paint used for the front door. This first textured element is such a lovely, stylish introduction to the home I couldn't resist it. The only issue using paint like this is that it is impossible to touch up. If it gets scratched or scuffed, it needs a whole new coat. The drama and shimmer of it though was totally worth it and a coat of paint on such a small area doesn't take all that long to do.

BRINGING COLOUR INTO THE HOME

Other coloured elements come in the form of the linen. Cushions are a fairly standard way to bring a pop of colour to sofas and beds alike, but coloured linen is another brilliant way to soften a room and add visual interest. I love to play around with different coloured fitted and top sheets, but keeping the same type and fibre. It's a bit like when you wear a pair of pants with a blazer to break up a suit – it's a great idea as long as you keep the fabrics the same. Changing fabrics can be problematic and lessen the result.

Bedcovers also add layers and interest, and in this home, it was a palette of blushes and greys that I favoured with lots of velvet thrown into the mix for some lovely luscious texture.

One of the rugs also had a big pop of navy blue. It's one of my favourite colours to use in interiors, so it was fitting that I included it in my own home's front sitting room. The white graduating into blue with the dip-dyed Hyam rug I created for my range was the perfect complement to the beautiful Megan Weston painting above the grey sofa. I'm so in love with the painting – it truly makes the room something special and is definitely the big drawcard of the room.

Adding an extra layer

Grey and white colour schemes sometimes need to be livened up to stop them looking lacklustre. Every space in the home required a different approach to the challenge of layering in interest, with texture and pattern of some sort being the solution in every case.

THE MASTER SUITE

The master bedroom has many beautiful elements, but on its own is a fairly standard room, with a standard ceiling height. It could have been delivered as just a plain Jane white room relying on the plantation shutters to add some charm, but, frankly, that just wouldn't do.

Grasscloth paper adorns three of the walls, the other left bare white for balance and a little breathing space. The white timberwork sits nicely against the wall coverings, popping the skirting and architraves for that little bit more drama and impact.

The texture and colour of the wall covering ties in beautifully with the sisal flooring that snakes its way down the stairs, and the textured elements from the stairs, and the lovely square panelled detail on all walls of the formerly fairly dull staircase, tie in well with the doors of the robes.

More texture is found in the ensuite, with the floor tile pattern and colour being the dramatic base for the crisp white and aged brass palette. The wall tiles are all about subtle texture rather than bold pattern or colour.

Below: Textural interest can be found in the grasscloth paper, cotton sheets, woven fabric bedhead and velvet bedcover.

FLOORING

The flooring downstairs is a lovely textured element too. It's easy, when you have pine flooring, to scowl at its yellow gaudiness and promptly stain it a dark colour, but my decision was to do almost the opposite. I wanted to expose the colour of the timber, not the lacquered oxidised yellow that everyone associates with pine floors, but the lovely sandy colour of the timber in its raw state.

Sanded back, the timber is truly beautiful, and the lines of the joins are accentuated by the natural lightness of the timber. The nail heads, perhaps seen by some as an eyesore, are lovely contrasting dots against the sandy raw base, and echo the knots in the timber. The whole expanse of flooring became elevated, and is one of my favourite things about the entire interior palette.

The travertine tiles with the beautiful, traditional French pattern were chosen to match the timber and, thankfully, the two sit beautifully side by side where they meet at the step up into the dining room. The pattern is interesting, the colour is perfect and the texture is visually warm and inviting, and perfectly in keeping with the contemporary take on a classic home style. The floors, too, are mercifully cool during summer and underfloor heating keeps your tootsies happy in the cooler months.

THE SMALL DETAILS THAT MAKE A DIFFERENCE

The wall tiles in the kitchen and in the laundry are the same as in the bathrooms, but the grout colour was changed from white to grey for more interest. It also gives the tiles a geometric pop that nicely matches in with the grey and the white parts of the kitchen.

Texture is added to the kitchen by way of the benchtop, originally planned to be Calacatta marble but it is, in fact, the more practical and cost-effective Caesarstone. The vein and white and grey contrast is the same as marble, but the product is more predictable and more durable.

The tapware is like the jewellery of this home, a really perfect element to add lustre and a sense of luxury to the wet rooms. Even the sink waste in the kitchen has the same lovely aged brass finish. These little elements, though quite considerable in terms of effort and expense to source, really do lift the bathrooms and kitchen from nice to amazing. Because you see them every day and touch them a lot, they are definitely some of those elements worth investing in to add an extra layer to your home.

Above: A modern rangehood sits discreetly above the stove.

Right: A pull-out cupboard allows easy access to everyday kitchen appliances.

Panelling hides the neighbouring property, and is a lovely thing to look at in itself. The spiral staircase leads up to a terraced area.

Focal points

Yes, art is the perfect focal point, and this home has some lovely art. I would have to say that, considering the collection is all mine, but it really makes the best of every room that it's used in.

The middle lounge room, being so simple and grey and white, is enlivened by the amazing neon colours of the Françoise Nielly piece we picked up on one of our trips to Paris. We happened to be walking past the gallery when we noticed one of her paintings hanging in the window. I'd seen her art a few years before on The Cool Hunter website, and it struck me as both graceful and impactful, a hard two to marry.

The art in this room is a mix of dearly loved and acquired pieces from our histories. There are three pieces – two figurative and one Aboriginal abstract – that you might not necessarily group together if you were doing design by numbers. That's the beauty of doing my own home, I don't mind so much what others think and I'm happy to include the pieces that light me up and get a response from my family on a day-to-day basis.

The light fittings in the home are also a major focal point which I've already talked about. You hopefully take note of these cues in a considered and resolved interior, but don't consciously realise their relevance. You feel, though, that the home feels 'right', without perhaps fully understanding why.

If I think about my favourite things in the home, they are possibly the things that stand out the most. I suppose that qualifies them as focal points, but they're more

Below: Found in a gallery in Paris, this Françoise Nielly painting lights up the otherwise white space.

Plants and flowers liven up any space, but it is important to match them to the style of your home.

Opposite: Soft and pretty hydrangeas work well with the traditional style of the home.

architectural in their nature. The ceilings, for example, I think are one of the superstars of this house, just as they are in all the other houses in the street that have retained them. The staircase, previously just a transition, is now something really stately and elegant with drama, impact, pattern, relief, texture, metal and movement all in one relatively confined space. It goes to show you what paying attention to the details of every space can do for the appeal of a home as this staircase, in my opinion, is definitely one of the main things that gets your attention when you arrive and sticks in your memory long after you leave.

DECORATION

My own home is a pretty easy problem to solve on the decorating front, because I have so many things acquired from projects, trips abroad and shopping adventures. I know that if I buy something I love, I will always find somewhere to put it, either in a client's home, my office or my home.

I still, though, have to choose the right pieces to complement the interior and bring all the disparate elements to life, creating that lived-in feel while making sure I don't go overboard on the tchotchkes in the process.

I layered in old candles and brand spanking new ones, freshened up the place with lovely diffusers with the scent of my favourite Jo Malone fragrance, Pomegranate Noir, and found plenty of opportunities for setting down succulents and orchids to layer in that natural living element.

Books are great for making you smart, and they're just as good, I think, for painting a picture of what you love, what's important to you and also giving you an opportunity to build neat little stacks that add interest to bookshelves, coffee tables and mantels.

Think about the towels you choose for your bathrooms at home. These elements can be décor items too. The towels in my place were flat and textured and perfectly suited to the rest of the home. Blue or green terry-towelling ones from a two dollar shop wouldn't have had the same effect.

We don't all live in photoshoots, and you can absolutely cycle through your towels and tea towels for convenience, but if you ever want to show your home at its best, don't forget about these little details.

Flowers also lift rooms. I have seen plenty of examples where a room comes to life with the right flowers, en masse. You don't need to get fussy, but do think about the type of flowers and whether they suit your style of home. I do this by feel, but it seems obvious to me that a sweet, traditional house would have sweet, traditional flowers such as hydrangeas, roses and peonies. Some more modern homes might call for natives or something a bit more obscure, so think about whether the flowers you really love will work with, or fight against, your chosen style. I used a mix of hydrangeas, Australian natives, roses and succulents in this house as they just felt as if they suited it.

I've renovated several homes, and have managed to live in some for a short length of time or, in some cases, not at all. When we fell in love with the Edgecliff house, it was supposed to be our family's five-year house. The idea was to improve it to make our lives better and more comfortable and, in a way that I didn't expect, that became the case.

We fell for another house in the period of time it took to renovate Edgecliff and, thankfully, due to the value added through consistent, considered design solutions, we were able to sell it and trade up to a lovely big home at Sydney's Bondi Beach.

The months of work, the effort, the challenges, the trials and triumphs all resulted in me passing on, in no time, yet another home to a new and passionate owner. That's the lot of a serial renovator, but it does mean there will be a new home project for me to sink my teeth into and share with you all soon enough.

Opposite: Books are great for creating a bedside table vignette, but don't be too precious about them – ultimately, they're there for reading, not styling!

Two living rooms are separated by a sliding door, allowing the front room to be turned into a cosy winter sitting room or even a guest bedroom.

Acknowledgements

Felix Forest, thanks for making the work look its best. I'm so glad I have been able to work with you – you're a superstar, and now everyone else knows what I've been able to see over our many shoots over many years. Thanks for being on board again.

To Louise, Steve, Cathy, Rob, Julian, Sarah, Cass and Alex, thank you for being in the book and for working with me to achieve your perfect homes.

To Olivier and Hugo, I am so grateful for you both. Chris, John, Michael, Jase, Rob, Pete, Baci, Reidy and Bahar, thanks for your ongoing support and friendship. And to all our family and all our friends, thank you for being part of my past, my present and my future. To John and Dayne, thank you for taking me under your wing and showing me the ropes way back when.

Alexandra and Adam, you're a great team to have behind me. Shane, Michelle, Amanda and Jaycie, so, too, are you. To Ania, Gabby, Kimberley, Peter, Renee and Renata, the shoots wouldn't have run so well if it weren't for your help, thank you. Scott, Darren and the Rolyon team, and Adam, Mark and all at Pivotal Constructions, thanks for working with me on your award-winning projects. Congratulations on your great work. Stacey K, thanks for being you. To Darron and Aimee, you guys are brilliant. Kris, Shannon and Dylan, I appreciate your expertise and assistance.

To Diana, Leta, Steve, Jane, Madeleine, Christine and Patty and everyone from Murdoch, thanks for making *Easy Luxury* the success it is and giving *HomeSpace* the same opportunity. Lisa Green, thank you for liking my voice and trusting it for the pages of *House & Garden*.

To Simpsons, thanks for having my back. Fi and Grahame, thank you. Rae, I wouldn't be the man I am today if it weren't for your support and wisdom. Jane and the team at Chic, I can't wait to see what we achieve together.

Julz, Dave, Juzzie, Scott, Shelley, Shaynna, Neale and all of the soundos, camera guys, producers and crew of *The Block*, it's always a pleasure to work with you. To all of my partners and suppliers, business partners and team members, thank you for getting behind me, staying in my corner and working with me to achieve great things. I'm proud of working with you all.

Thank you to my suppliers for assisting me continuously with my work and these photoshoots: Academy Brand, Adairs, Adam Dixon, Armadillo & Co, Arteriors, Astra Walker, Audi, Bandhini, Beaumonts, Becker Minty, Boyd Blue, Cadrys, Calibre, Carpet Court, Catapult, Coco Republic, Cromwell, Cultiver, Designer Boys, Di Lorenzo, Dulux, Eadie Lifestyle, EcoSmart, English Tapware Co, Fabric Pavilion, Formrite, Freedom, Freedom Kitchens and the Kitchen Group, Garden Life, Glasshouse, Globe West, Good Guys, Horgans, Incy Interiors, Jo Malone, Legend, Lilly & Lolly, Linen House, Martin Browne Contemporary, MCM House, MRD Home, My Brother Albert, Orient House, Orson & Blake, Otomys, Out Deco, Planet Furniture, Pottery Barn, Radford Furnishings, Reece, RPD, Satara, Scandinavian Wallpaper & Décor, Schots, Seneca, Sheridan, Sounds Like Home, Stegbar, The Artwork Stylist, Thonet, Typo, Uniqwa, Unitex, Urban Couture, Velux, West Elm, Wet Design, Weylandts, Zakkia.

Murdoch Books would like to thank the following artists whose work appears in the pages of *HomeSpace*.
31 Polly Ngale. 41 Simon Taylor. 43 Sarrita King. 61 Fred Cress. 62–3 Fred Cress. 76 Geoffrey Proud. 78 Emma Hack. 81 Brett Whiteley. 85 Fred Cress. 102–135 Fred Cress. 149 Idris Murphy, Brett Whiteley. 154 Simeon Walker. 156 Damien Butler. 160–1 Isaac Julien. 164–5 David Aspden. 167 Newell Harry. 170 Tim Maguire. 176–7 Yumutjin Wunungmurra, Malaluba Gumana, Dhurrumuway Marika. 193 Megan Weston. 199 Sarrita King. 213 McLean Edwards. 217 Dorothy Napangardi. 220 Designer Boys. 228 Françoise Nielly.

Published in 2016 by Murdoch Books, an imprint of Allen & Unwin

Murdoch Books Australia
83 Alexander Street, Crows Nest NSW 2065
Phone: +61 (0)2 8425 0100
murdochbooks.com.au
info@murdochbooks.com.au

Murdoch Books UK
Ormond House, 26–27 Boswell Street, London WC1N 3JZ
Phone: +44 (0) 20 8785 5995
murdochbooks.co.uk
info@murdochbooks.co.uk

For corporate orders and custom publishing contact our business
development team at salesenquiries@murdochbooks.com.au

Publisher: Diana Hill
Editorial Manager: Jane Price
Design Manager: Madeleine Kane
Editor: Leta Keens
Designer: Stephen Smedley
Photographer: Felix Forest
Production Manager: Alexandra Gonzalez

ISBN 978 1 74336 703 2 Australia
ISBN 978 1 74336 736 0 UK
A cataloguing-in-publication entry is available from the catalogue
of the National Library of Australia at nla.gov.au
A catalogue record for this book is available from the British Library

Colour reproduction by Splitting Image Colour Studio Pty Ltd,
Clayton, Victoria
Printed by Hang Tai Printing Company Limited, China